MW00807466

The Craft of Clarity

SIX STEPS TO BRIDGE GAPS, FOSTER COMMITMENT, AND CREATE SUSTAINABLE ALIGNMENT

Casey Watts

Principal Principles Publications

United States of America

Contents

Table of Contents

Yes. Clear is kind.

But creating clarity is more than a moment- it's a leadership habit we build daily. It's the work of aligning people, cutting the noise, and turning potential into progress.

Because in leadership, clarity always precedes capacity.

-Casey

Acknowledgements

To Clif, my husband, who inspired this work and continuously encouraged me with one simple question and response: "How do you eat an elephant? One bite at a time." Your steady belief in me has been the fuel behind every word in this book.

To April, Jeri, and Suzanne—my CIA crew—you were the team I always searched for, and I'll forever be grateful for the bond we share. You knew exactly when to encourage, when to hug, when to poke fun, and when to laugh. I'll always be your Schiz.

To Alyssa, who endured and encouraged every Marco Polo rant and served as my biggest accountability partner, cheerleader, and thought provoker. You've kept me grounded and moving forward when I needed it most.

To Allison, who prepared me for this writing journey and stood as my prayer warrior through it all. Your faith and encouragement have been a constant source of strength.

To Michelle, the school leader who brought my ideas to life better than I could have imagined and gave words to concepts I wasn't quite ready to articulate. Your leadership and implementation of the Clarity Cycle Framework have been an incredible inspiration.

To my family who endured my hours of focus on research, writing, and revision to make this book a reality. Your patience, love, and understanding have meant everything.

And to you, reader—I am honored you have picked up this book with the hopes of bridging student learning gaps, fostering commitment from your people, and creating sustainable alignment on your campus. You are deserving of my praise and so much more!

Not Another Unrealistic Book of Complicated Ideas

Intermundium: The World Between

Have you ever read a novel or series that transitions between characters every chapter or few chapters? Some people really love these novels and some people would rather read anything else at all! If you know the kind of novel I'm talking about, then you know that the reader exists on the outside. It's almost as though the reader lives in the in-between world of these characters. They get to see multiple perspectives, and thus, have an advantage of knowing and understanding more. Authors often call this world in between the "intermundium."

In education, there are also multiple worlds—most notably, the world of teachers and the world of leaders. I've lived in both, but I've also spent much of my time in the intermundium, moving between teachers, leaders, and other departments. That in-between space— where you get to travel across perspectives—is fascinating. Like reading a novel from multiple character viewpoints, it provides a broader understanding of both sides. But while it's interesting, it can also be frustrating and disheartening.

From this vantage point, I've noticed recurring, often opposing narratives from teachers and leaders. Here's a glimpse:

TEACHER:

- *"We never know what's going on..."*
- *"I'm so confused..."*
- *"I'm just gonna do me..."*

LEADER:

- *"No one will get on board..."*
- *"Everyone is all over the place..."*
- *"They just go back to their classrooms and make no changes..."*

There are countless situations where these misaligned perspectives surface. Let's take a closer look at these different situations and the opposing perspectives.

Teacher	Situation	Leader
"Great, another thing to add to the plate that they'll just change again..."	New curriculum, program, or initiative	*"We're not adding more to their plates— if anything, this should feel like less of a load..."*
"I don't understand what they want from us with this new curriculum. What does 'fidelity' even mean?"	Implementation confusion	*"We're not seeing everyone implement this with fidelity, even though we made that an expectation..."*
"They keep saying, 'We're dedicated to high-quality Tier 1 instruction,' but no one's told us what that looks like."	Tier 1 instructional strategies	*"They're still relying on whole-group lectures as their primary mode of instruction..."*
"When are we supposed to have time to actually do this? We can't meet during conference time..."	Teachers receive training on analyzing assessment data	*"They can dedicate at least one conference period or a planning block each nine weeks to get this done..."*

Figure 0.1

Of course, no teacher or leader sets out to create chaos. No one wakes up thinking, "How can I make life harder for everyone so we stay on this hamster wheel forever?" But somehow, despite good intentions, this misalignment persists. Teachers feel frustrated, left in the dark about expectations. Leaders feel equally frustrated when their teams seem reluctant to engage or adapt.

If, like me, you've spent time in the intermundium—navigating the space between these roles—you've probably felt like you were flipping channels between two competing storylines. And I don't know about you, but I feel a deep responsibility to bridge this gap. It's time to sew these two worlds together so that the same story is being written.

Bridging the Gap and Building Commitment

There are usually two different stories at play when campus or district leaders try to get teachers and staff to "buy in," only to encounter what looks like resistance. But what if the issue isn't about "buy-in" at all? What if bridging the gap is really about alignment and building a culture of commitment rather than compliance?

In their book, School Culture Rewired, Gruenert and Whitaker (2015) describe culture as a school's personality and climate as its attitude. I believe that when leaders push for buy-in, what they're really working on is climate—something rooted in feelings and attitudes. But feelings fluctuate, and if leadership's focus remains on buy-in, the two worlds—teachers and leaders—will continue to operate on separate tracks, each with its own narrative. True alignment requires more than attitude shifts. It requires a culture change.

The dictionary defines commitment as the state or quality of being dedicated to a cause. I say that commitment means we strive toward a shared purpose even when it's hard to buy in emotionally. When we're committed, we don't just follow along because we feel good about something—we stick with it because we believe in the greater goal. This kind of commitment is what binds teams together and keeps them moving forward, even through discomfort or doubt.

When I first committed myself to bridging the gap between these two worlds—leaders and teachers—I knew it would take more than good intentions. It would require being strategic, intentional, and supremely responsive. If I wanted aligned teams that were committed, I needed to approach the challenge thoughtfully. But honestly? It felt overwhelming, if not impossible. "How do I get everyone on the same page? How do we, in the words of General Stanley McChrystal (2015), get them 'all to be bound by a sense of common purpose'?"

As my husband always says, "How do you eat an elephant? One bite at a time." And so, I took what felt like the first bite—the first step.

The Origin Story: The Aspiring Leader's Quest

I didn't follow any one protocol initially. But I found myself devouring leadership books. Organizational leadership has always fascinated me, so that part was quite enjoyable. I culled and implemented ideas from thought leaders like Andy Stanley, Peter DeWitt, Simon Sinek, Chip Heath, Dan Heath, and John Maxwell, just to name a few.

Then one day, a classroom teacher, who was working toward her Master's and Principal's certificate, asked me, "How did you do it? How did you start getting everyone on the same page and moving in the same direction?" It surprised me to hear someone ask that. It's what we had been working toward for such a long time. But hearing those words said aloud—those exact words—is something I'll never forget. When people begin to notice alignment and collective commitment, even in small ways, it means something essential has been provided.

Did I know at the time that what we were providing was **clarity**? Not at all. So, when this aspiring leader asked, "How did you get everyone on the same page?" my first response was, "Well, I just zoomed out to see the bigger picture and then zoomed back in to figure out how we could help everyone move forward together."

Thankfully, she didn't accept that pitiful answer. She wanted the details, the nitty-gritty. She was determined to learn, grow, and prepare for the work of leading as a future principal.

Out of this aspiring leader's quest to grow (and others' genuine curiosity about how to get everyone in the same boat, rowing in the same direction), I was able to map out the steps we took to bridge the gap between leaders and teachers. These steps aligned PLCs and teams—teams that moved confidently in unison toward a common focus.

From this quest, the **Clarity Cycle Framework** was born.

Not Another Unrealistic Book of Ideas...

The Clarity Cycle Framework has now been utilized in dozens of campuses and districts and counting! Leaders and leadership teams have used the Clarity Cycle Framework:

- When starting a new campus or improving a turnaround campus

- To streamline and implement high-quality Tier 1 instruction (and decrease the numbers of students in Tiers 2 and 3)

- When rolling out a new curriculum or initiative

- To support their district and campus strategic plan goals

- As a way to develop PLCs (that are actual professional learning communities and not planning meetings)

- For developing customized observation forms that are meaningful to teachers

- To develop school-wide culture routines

- When considering how to help teachers with materials and lesson internalization

And the list goes on!

Why is it catching on? Well, I'd like to boldly say that the strategy itself is very simple: know where you are, know where you're going, and create a plan to get there. But your strategy to get everyone moving in the same direction is only as effective as the clarity that you bring to the strategy— and clarity is QUITE complex!

Now, let me assure you, even though creating clarity is complex, the actual framework I'm writing about was never meant to be so, nor was it meant to be a set of unrealistic ideas that sound good in theory. I believe that maintaining simplicity is absolutely necessary, especially in the education world. There are too many things on leaders' and teachers' plates to implement another novel or lofty approach. The Clarity Cycle Framework takes the complexity of clarity and makes it manageable and actionable! This is where you are going to see collective efficacy come to life!

It's like asking my teenage boys to clean a room. My sons' versions of "clean" and my version of "clean" are two very different things. I can't just tell them, "Go clean the kitchen," and expect magic to happen. If I want them to clean effectively, I need to do what Brené Brown (2018) calls, "paint done." I need to clearly explain what needs to be cleaned, what areas need the most attention, and why it matters. I also have to outline specific steps they could take from start to finish and offer meaningful praise and encouragement along the way.

So it is with our teams—if we want them to have a common collective focus, to pave a path, and to all move in the same direction so we can increase teacher capacity and shrink learning gaps, then we MUST provide a great deal of clarity, and we must do so strategically!

I come to this work with more than 20 years of experience in education as a classroom teacher, instructional leader, coach, and consultant. While I hold various degrees and certifications, the heart of the **Clarity Cycle Framework** comes from real-world, boots-on-the-ground experience. I've seen firsthand what works—and what doesn't. The framework has grown out of both successes and failures.

Now, can I sit here and tell you that the Clarity Cycle will be the key to making your vision and dreams come true? That teacher capacity will skyrocket, retention will stabilize, and student learning will grow by leaps and bounds after implementation? No, of course not. It's like asking my boys to clean the kitchen—just because I provide explicit, detailed instructions doesn't guarantee the kitchen will turn out the way I envisioned. There is no magic bullet, no enchanted vase we can rub to make all our challenges disappear.

The truth is, that worthwhile change takes effort and sustained attention. When we constantly search for a quick fix, we rob ourselves of the opportunity to develop the habits and mindsets needed to make meaningful change stick. Real progress comes from honing the art of leadership—the kind of leadership that brings so much clarity to a vision that alignment seems to happen naturally.

When people eventually start asking you, "How did you do it? How did you get everyone on the same page and moving forward together?" you'll know that it wasn't just because you followed a framework. It's because you cultivated the mindsets and habits of a leader who has mastered the craft of clarity.

Part 1: The Why

CHAPTER 1

Quiet Chaos

Why did we do this?

I'm in the driver's seat, rolling my neck this way and that in an attempt to release the tension starting to build up. I'm trying my best to focus on the road and ignore the feeling of inner chaos- you know, the kind of inner turmoil that has your stomach churning, your temples throbbing, and the thought, "*Why did we do this?*" playing on repeat in your mind.

A couple of years back, my family and I went on a big family vacation. It was our "experience gift" to our kids for Christmas. We purchased walking sticks for them to unwrap, t-shirts with the words "Grand Canyon" printed on the back, and nice water packs. Yes, we had plans to go to the Grand Canyon, but it was going to be so much more than just the Grand Canyon we would see. In fact, my husband and I had mapped out an entire seven-day road trip to visit a whopping six National Parks out west! It involved long hours of driving, lots of hiking, and several different hotels. I won't go into all the details of this "Watts Tour of National Parks" (however, I will say you can compare it to National Lampoon's Vacation, minus the exaggerated and sometimes criminal mishaps). But I *am* going to ask you to empathize with me for a moment.

You see, we're parents of three children. One thing we all know about children, even if you're not currently a parent yourself, is that they ask a lot of questions, especially when traveling: "When will we be there? What time is it? Are we almost there?," ... just to name a few. One of our children, in particular, has the genius of Wonder,[1] which means he takes great joy in wondering about anything and everything. While the two teens in the car were absorbed in their devices and blissfully unaware of their surroundings, this preteen wondered, questioned, and made every detail in his mind known to the public. For the first three or four hours of the trip, we only barely endured the barrage of questions. I can't speak for my husband, but I can confidently say that the one question fluttering of its own accord through my mind was, *"WHY DID WE DO THIS?"*

While there wasn't a *visible* chaos of temper tantrums or flailing, a *quiet chaos* was felt internally by us all—my son included. Imagine for a moment, if you will, what we were failing to recognize about our son, and quite honestly human nature. Imagine what kind of confusion and anxiety we were causing for him simply because we hadn't found the right way to bring clarity to the situation. From his perspective, it was probably like being trapped in a net of unanswered questions, unable to claw his way out. He was likely as frustrated with us as we were with him, especially considering how his siblings had joined in on the snippy responses. When we realized that the questions wouldn't stop until we provided the right kind of clarity, we took a different approach.

Instead of snapping back or ignoring him completely, we created a daily schedule with tentative times. We pulled up a map and explained where we would notice a change in time zones. We showed pictures of the different hotels we'd be staying in and discovered which ones had pools and which didn't, as well as how much time there would actually be to swim once we arrived. And it was okay that everything was tentative, because we had brought **clarity** to the destinations and the small steps to getting there. Even when things changed, there was a calm that wouldn't have existed before.

Now, it's probably common sense to provide that kind of clarity to a child. We definitely could have saved ourselves a whole heap of trouble had we done that to begin with. But we made the assumption

---

[1] Working Genius Assessment

that, because our children were pre-teens or teens, we could forgo proactive clarity building work.

The Dream versus The Reality

The Dream

Before going on this family vacation, we imagined sunny skies, easy conversation, no traffic, smiles, and laughter. Isn't this what we all tend to do? We imagine what could be and what we believe SHOULD be of any given situation—vacations, new jobs, marriage, having children—you name it.

The same is true for us as instructional leaders. We want great things for our schools. We imagine in our PLCs and teams a kind of calm that, even when things change, we can collectively pivot together and still be ready and eager to provide the best instruction possible for our students. More than that, though, what we want is for people to be part of teams that move forward, make an impact together, and leave them feeling empowered, inspired, and essential. If we dig deep enough, we all may realize that this is how capacity is built and where collective efficacy is realized. This is how we retain great teachers who maintain full engagement and function in "the flow."

When I began presenting at conferences on the idea of aligned professional learning communities (PLCs) and teams, I knew it would be important to consider and showcase teachers' perceptions. The question I pondered was, "What do teachers REALLY think about PLCs and team meetings and WHY?" One of the best places to go to get unfiltered opinions, of course, is social media platforms. I investigated several educator Facebook groups and simply typed "PLC" in the search bar of each group. The results were fascinating! I spent hours scrolling, screenshotting, highlighting, and taking notes about what I discovered.

In Figure 1.1, I've highlighted some of the positive comments that stood out among the search. Only a couple are included in this book because, well, there weren't many to choose from. These are the kinds of comments of which we dream and would love to see more of from teachers and staff.

PLCs changed me as a teacher. I have direction and intentionality behind my decisions now. Plan together, share the workload, and treat the students as "your students."

🖒 2

A PLC is an ongoing, long-term process of collaboration and reflection.

Figure 1.1

"PLCs changed me as a teacher." Wow. How often do we hear that? Not often enough. When I read these comments, it gives me hope. PLCs and teams that people are eager to meet with *can* actually exist. One can't help but wonder, though, how the environments these teachers had experienced came to be. How is it that they were able to be fully engaged and committed?

The Reality

I wish there were a plethora of positive comments like those shown in Figure 1.1. There's a different reality at play, though, and the comments below are often what we might experience instead. Beware—these comments may elicit strong feelings for any number of reasons depending on your role and your past experiences with PLCs.

Our PLCs are actually just department meetings

Not a fan, but I could be if we were allowed the professional courtesy of talking about what we need to talk about, but that's not the case. We have to address data and we have an overwhelmingly long PLC form to fill out each week. It's just another hoop we have to jump through. We get virtually nothing out of it.

🖒 8

They are a total waste of time. Let teachers teach. Give them the info via email or a handout, but stop wasting our time!

🖒 6

I think our definitions of PLCs may be different as how you are describing them sound different. My experience of them is just the coaches or admin running a meeting that could be an email that takes up a planning period that could actually be put to better use of actually planning for students, catching up on grading, etc. instead of listening to what could be an email.

6

Figure 1.2

For many, these comments are not only applicable to PLCs—they can be said for faculty meetings, professional development sessions, planning days, data digs, and any other time meant for teams to collaborate intentionally. "A total waste of time." Well, isn't that disheartening? It's disheartening on multiple levels. Instructional leadership teams put their heart, soul, and mind into crafting meaningful experiences for teams. To know that people feel this way about the things we have arranged, hoping to impact students' lives, is crushing. As a fellow colleague once said, "*Why do I even try?*" It's disheartening for teachers as well, especially those that came into this profession longing to be a difference maker. And it's mostly disheartening for the students whose learning experiences are at stake when teams lack collective efficacy.

What's vitally important is that instructional leaders never lose sight of the dream, even when reality tries to get the best of us. Keeping sight of and striving for the dream requires a great deal of attention to the work that matters. You are one step ahead of the game simply by reading this book. If you are reading these words, you have what it takes to create focused and aligned teams that are fully engaged and "in the flow."

Fully Engaged and "In the Flow"

In his book, *The Five Disciplines of PLC Leaders* (2011), Timothy D. Kanold writes a full chapter about becoming a PLC leader with the discipline of reflection and balance, one who can engage fully in their work and take deliberate breaks to rest and recharge. This is important not just for PLC leaders, though. It's important for any leader and all team members. One might say that this is true for anyone who wants to experience fulfillment at work, and I highly recommend digging into Kanold's book if this describes you.

While it may be up to an individual to develop the discipline of reflection and balance so they can eagerly engage at work, we, as instructional leaders, absolutely have the duty to cultivate team environments that make this possible. In the next chapter, I'll be exploring an adaptation of Kanold's (2011) PLC energy quadrant that showcases what is needed in order for whole teams, not just individuals, to experience alignment, engagement, and empowerment. It can be thought of as an additional layer to the PLC Energy Quadrant. So, let's take a moment to briefly reference Kanold's work and Figure 1.3.

The PLC Energy Quadrants

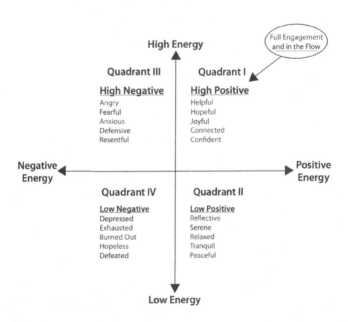

Figure 1.3 Reprinted from Kanold, T. D. (2011). *The Five Disciplines of PLC Leaders.* Bloomington, IN: Solution Tree Press.

Kanold (2011) created the PLC energy quadrants from the work of Loehr and Schwartz (2003) in their book *The Power of Full Engagement*. In this quadrant, he explores the energy exertion from a PLC leader, noting that the highest functioning leader lives between Quadrant I and Quadrant II. As can be seen in this graphic, one who can achieve this will be highly engaged and "in the flow," while also maintaining a reflective and peaceful nature. They might be seen as natural-born leaders, but we know there is no such thing. Becoming this kind of person takes time, effort, and intention. Building the kind of environment where our colleagues can live between these quadrants takes incredibly MORE time, effort, and intention.

It is more than evident that the teachers who made such positive comments about PLCs (see Figure 1.1) had been afforded the space, time, and clarity to function between Quadrants I and II of the positive energy quadrant. These individuals undoubtedly have high capacity. They are the people leaders seek to hire and keep. They become the people we believe will create "dream teams" in our schools.

On the other hand, the teachers who made such negative comments about PLCs (see Figure 1.2) had not YET experienced the kind of environments that led them to a high energy, high positive state. They are part of teams that live in Quadrants III and IV. Members of these teams permeate resistance and toxicity. It's not because they aim to do so. It is not their intent to hold teams back from developing collective efficacy and becoming a "dream team," nor is it their intent to be the kind of person that leaders prefer not to hire or keep. Then what is it? Why do so many teams, if it's not their intent, function in high negative and low negative quadrants that deplete capacity? Why do so many teams continue to live in a world of resentment, burnout, and chaos?

I have personal experience with a majority of teams living in these undesirable energy quadrants, where chaos permeated the culture. When we envision this kind of culture, it can be easy to think of the Tazmanian devil swirling about loudly and making a mess of everything in his path. But let me be clear– this is often not the kind of chaos we notice in schools. Instead, it's more of a quiet chaos, much like the quiet chaos that overtook our minivan during our National Parks adventure.

Quiet Chaos in Schools

In this book, you'll notice phrases and terms such as "quiet chaos," "misalignment," "faux collaboration," and of course, "the craft of clarity." Because while a few positive Facebook posts may give us hope that collaborative alignment can exist, it is rarely the case. Let me be clear, not all schools have this problem. But I will venture to say that more often than not, schools and teams function without clarity around a common focus. Instead, a quiet chaos persists without being addressed. Perhaps the following story will illuminate what I mean by "quiet chaos."

Before I dive into this story, I want to be sure I'm not alone here. Go ahead and admit (and just for the record, I'm imagining that you're boldly admitting this) that you have a close colleague with whom you've engaged in private chats during "certain" meetings– informational Zoom meetings, district administration meetings, the dreaded after-work faculty meetings, and sometimes even team planning meetings! Don't worry, you're not alone. I'd like to be vulnerable enough in this book to share my own private conversation with a colleague that was carried out completely by GIFs (you know the kind).

You might be imagining your own personal contexts for this GIF conversation. This is my context: There I am, sitting in a third-grade classroom amidst a team of teachers during their team meeting. It was a typical, weekly Thursday team meeting. Team members were spread about the room in a haphazard way, some with notebooks, some with laptops, some with nothing but their person in tow, and all facing the screen at the front of the empty classroom. But this time, even if the physical structure didn't contribute to a collaborative professional learning community, I was expecting things to be quite different.

You see, just a week before, I had spent time coaching the administrator regarding team meetings and the collective PLC. She was more than ready to move teams in the right direction and wanted collaboration to improve. As I eagerly coached her with intentional questions, she came to the idea of expecting team leads to craft an agenda for each team meeting. It was simple, but it was a start that we hoped would move the needle. She made the announcement to teachers during a faculty meeting. Maybe it wasn't with much conviction, and maybe it wasn't with a solid "why" behind it, but the announcement was made and the expectation set nonetheless. The following week, the first planning meetings, where agendas were expected, took place.

Boy, was I excited! I couldn't wait to see what the agendas entailed and how this collaborative time might be different—FINALLY, more productive, more engaging, more life-giving! I took my seat in the third-grade classroom, prepared for the moment!

After the five teachers claimed their self-assigned seats (in the same haphazard way mentioned above), the team lead placed the agenda under the document camera to display on the board for all to see. Now, you can imagine my pure defeat and deflation when what my eyes witnessed was a scratch sheet of notebook paper with three measly bullet points. While I am only somewhat ashamed to have taken a picture of the "agenda" on the sly, it feels more appropriate and respectful to type out this agenda below instead of displaying the picture for all the world to see:

Team Agenda:
- Lesson plans
- Grades
- Copies

And so, the day continued, in this same way, for at least five of the seven teams. Not only were the agendas lackluster, but they also were accompanied with looks of disdain, discomfort, and sometimes sarcastic humor. No one outrightly commented about this small little agenda initiative, but the negative mindsets could be felt, seen, and more than likely heard in whispers behind closed doors. This is one element of *"quiet chaos,"* internal personal chaos—a stirring of emotions that remain suppressed and hushed, only expressed to colleagues who share similar emotions or are unwilling to go against the grain, even if they are a proponent of an initiative or change. This quiet chaos affects the culture of the school because the toxicity of these emotions is manifested in teachers' and leaders' actions.

There's another element of "quiet chaos," though, and one that this book serves to illuminate and cure—it's one of internal organizational chaos. It is the primary cause of internal personal chaos. Webster's dictionary defines chaos as "complete disorder and confusion." Internal organizational chaos is most easily witnessed from a birds' eye view. It looks similar to an anthill that has been knocked over and scattered, ants scurrying about in all different directions attempting to work toward the same goal but failing to create one cohesive mound. Sometimes fire ants will build mounds on the edges of our driveway. My son recently decided to spray one of the larger anthills with water, which caused ants to scatter everywhere. We could see the internal organizational chaos he had created, but it could not be heard. It was quiet. It was continuous.

And so it was with the teams who had been encouraged to create agendas. Even after agendas were implemented week after week, the meetings continued as they always had, with limited focus, limited effort, and limited positive results in student learning and engagement of staff. Instead of functioning as a team of teams, as schools should function, it was as though everyone was working in their own silos— meeting simply to add meaningless words to lesson plans, heading back to classrooms to close doors and do "what's best for my own students," dreading planning meetings and "PLC meetings" (or meetings of any kind for that matter), and **struggling with the same problems over and over again, year after year**.

Rest assured; a school can appear to function well even amidst quiet chaos. Those who have never experienced anything different might *believe* they are part of a school with focused and productive teams. This perception can be shared by team members, as well as campus and district instructional leaders. Teams may seem to get along, lesson plans will be completed, and test scores might even reflect "success." The community may feel satisfied with what they believe is happening within the school. However, a leader who recognizes that this is not the case—that the school is actually suffering from underlying chaos—will act quickly to address it. We might notice these leaders attempting to set clear agendas for meetings, implementing consistent curricula or programs, or introducing a range of strategic solutions.

Let's be honest, the internal organizational chaos I described earlier didn't occur because we lacked a solid agenda. It wasn't due to a lack of strategy either. In fact, we believed we had a great strategy—we understood the starting point of these meetings, knew where we wanted them to go, and had a plan to get there, complete with agendas. As "drivers," it's easy to get frustrated and think, "Someone on each team could have and should have stepped up to craft a meaningful agenda." But it was crucial for us to step back and consider why they didn't. If we had a straightforward strategy for aligning these teams and guiding them toward positive, high-energy outcomes, then what was it that we, as leaders, did—or didn't do—that prevented these teams from succeeding?

Here's the thing … While strategy can be quite simple, clarity is immensely complex, and CLARITY is what we lacked.

CHAPTER 2

Strategy is Simple.
Clarity is Complex.

The Limitations of Strategy

In the animated movie *Zootopia*, a hyper bunny and sly fox rush to the DMV to gather crucial information for solving a crime. To the bunny's frustration, the workers are all sloths, moving at, well ... a sloth's pace. What should have been a quick task turns into a painfully slow ordeal. This scene felt all too real when I recently took my son to the DMV to get his learner's permit. My strategy was simple: download the list of required items, gather them in a folder, and head to the DMV—easy, right? Not quite.

Despite our preparation, we missed a few details. After waiting 45 minutes, we found out we hadn't checked in properly and had to wait even longer. Then, at the counter, we were told our documents were incomplete, requiring a second trip. Eventually, after much hassle, we finally walked out with the permit. My son's reflection said it all: "I feel like we've just been in that scene from *Zootopia* with the sloth at the DMV."

Strategy itself is very simple: figure out where you are, figure out where you are going, and create a plan to get there. Seems easy, right? But there is another layer. As you likely know, the problems we encounter that require strategy can be supremely complex. So strategy alone doesn't actually solve the problem. Case in point, I had everything I needed (in theory) to get my son's permit. I could even visualize the process. But, in actuality, it was much more complex.

Schools are no stranger to complex problems. They also are no stranger to strategic plans (be them good or bad) to solve those problems. Let's take a step back and think about the mountain of problems we might notice in schools across the state, nation, and world:

- Unproductive and pointless "PLCs"
- Lackluster team meetings
- High turnover
- Resistance to change initiatives
- Low attendance rates
- Plummeting test scores
- Struggling readers
- Significant behavior issues
- Uninvolved parents and guardians
- Tier 1 instruction is lacking or nonexistent
- And the list goes on, right?

In fact, we can even drill down each of those and create lengthy sublists. And for each item on those lists, leaders may either proactively or reactively create solutions in the form of strategy alone. We know where we are, we know where we are going or would like to go, and we create a plan to get there. Consider the problem so often noticed in MTSS or RTI. Gaps in learning are increasing along with numbers of students in Tiers 2 and 3. We aim to close those learning gaps through Tiers 1, 2, and 3 instruction. To do so, we plan to purchase and implement products and programs to support students in Tiers 2 and 3 (Figure 2.1).

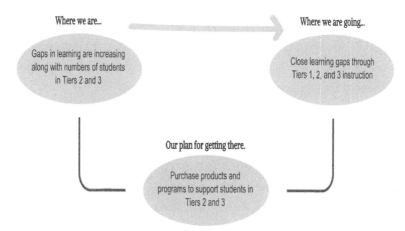

Figure 2.1

Isn't it interesting, though, that the problem often remains, and we end up pondering why this strategy isn't working? We can see this with other common school problems as well. Low attendance rates are met with the strategy of attendance initiatives that are short-lived. Unproductive teams are provided strict agendas as a strategy to get them on track, but team members seem resistant and resentful. Upticks in behavior issues have us grasping at straws, such as extrinsic rewards systems that do little to change behaviors.

Speaking of initiatives—that seems to be a consistent strategy for solving widespread, cyclical problems. But you know how *that* goes—leaders either "mandate" initiatives and attempt to hold people accountable (which turns into micromanagement), or push the pause button because people "aren't ready for it" (which turns into neglect and one failed initiative after another). You see, strategy itself is quite simple, but it's definitely not enough.

Anyone Can Strategize

In fact, anyone can create a strategy for navigating their way out of a problem. Anyone can create a strategic plan for their campus or district. Anyone can determine a vision for their organization or their team. Anyone can craft a set of goals. Anyone can create a *plan* for bringing that vision to life and reaching goals.

We see it all the time. Campuses and districts pull together small teams to refresh vision and mission statements, develop strategic and improvement plans, or set instructional goals for the year. Leaders often spend hours or even days filling out multi-page improvement plan templates. As I write this, I have a District Improvement Plan from a small rural district beside me—forty-nine pages long! One of the Campus Improvement Plans is twenty-one pages. While some leaders might treat these plans as items to "check off the list," I believe most have noble intentions to make their plans and goals truly matter.

But even with the best intentions, strategic plans and initiatives very rarely come to fruition or are very rarely sustained. In fact, statistics show that between 60-90% of strategic plans fail (Olsen, 2022). What we notice as a result is the quiet chaos I mentioned in the last chapter. We notice teams, and individuals moving about in a million and one different directions, almost as though they are functioning in complete silos.

Strategy Doesn't Eliminate Silos

Several years ago, I served as a district instructional specialist in a medium-sized rural district. My role consisted of supporting principals and teachers in understanding and implementing current, best practices and utilizing curricular resources. It became apparent very quickly that alignment of pedagogy, practices, and curriculum was severely missing. David Ruddle, in his 2019 article for *Head Teacher Update*, summed up my experience perfectly:

> *Consistency is often a misconstrued word in education. It should not mean we want staff to be clones of each other—rather we want consistency in approaches and teachers working as teams rather than in silos. When I walked into a classroom, and spoke with individual teachers, it was like being in several different schools—it was not about getting consistency of the "style" of teaching, but of the same strategies, and pedagogical approach.*

We know that learning is a change in long-term memory—learning happens and needs to be consolidated over time (McCrea, 2018). Therefore, if teachers are using wildly different approaches, students will not benefit. For pupils to benefit, their learning needs to be built on prior knowledge, not be completely different each year. (paras 5-6)

The lack of consistency from classroom to classroom, grade level to grade level, and campus to campus was mind-boggling and caused an almost imperceptible chaos, but an undeniable disconnect both in adults and in students. Because no common language was being spoken and no common instructional focus was shared, learning gaps widened each year. The hard part about it was that these gaps were completely unintentional. Teachers and staff worked tirelessly day in and day out to support students and close gaps. I mean, obviously, no one *wants* gaps to happen. These teachers wanted the best for their students, or at least for their efforts to be recognized as a result of student learning.

For me, the thought of unintentional learning gaps happening simply because we weren't aligned was too much to handle. Of course, as an eager instructional leader, my instinct was to dive head first into solving this problem. After all, I knew where we were, I knew what we all wanted (to close learning gaps), and I decided that the strategy would be to focus teams on a framework for instruction that I believed would effectively move us all forward in one direction and, thus, close gaps. But because strategy itself isn't enough, my approach to solving this problem only added to the quiet chaos that was already at play and it definitely didn't eliminate the silos that existed within the school.

Nor will a simple plan to implement an initiative eliminate silos. In a 2024 ASCD blog post, David James wrote about designing strategic elementary schedules. He makes the valid point that even with strategic scheduling, silos can still exist. The example he gives is an elementary school principal strategizing the schedule to ensure that all teachers included 90 minutes of literacy instruction within the school day. The principal allowed teachers to choose where this 90 minutes would fall and what the 90 minutes would look like instructionally. But this strategy is flawed. Here's what James states:

> "*All these teachers are honoring the 90 minutes scheduled for literacy—yet they all spend the time in different ways, with **likely significant differences in learning and outcomes for students as a result.**" (emphasis mine)*

You see, the silos still exist and students bear the brunt of our strategic plans gone wrong. Or perhaps a strategic plan hasn't gone wrong, but it hasn't gone anywhere at all. These plans, too, serve only to magnify the silos where nothing but faux collaboration is happening—the complete opposite of collective efficacy. Teachers close their doors and do what they believe is best for their students.

But silos are not reserved only for teachers. Any stakeholder can become siloed. Special education teachers and interventionists work as best they can to meet the needs of their heavy caseloads, even when they have limited capacity to know what's going on in the classroom; administrators' time is filled with things keeping them in their offices versus in classrooms and team meetings; students are confused by the differences from teacher to teacher, classroom to classroom, and school to school. Even parents and community members can feel alone and confused.

So, What's the Real Challenge?

This doesn't make sense, does it? If strategy is so simple (figure out where you are, figure out where you are going, and create a plan to get there), then what causes strategic plans to fail? Why are so many problems cyclical? Why are initiatives short-lived? For most leaders, it's not strategy they are lacking. It's something else. Now, I hate to keep you waiting, but before we dig into this "something else" that's missing, I'd like to prime you by investigating one simple question, probably the most important question of all:

How often do we fail to remember that we are working in a PEOPLE business?

It's never up to one person to develop and execute strategy, although it might be nice if we could just snap our fingers and have everything fall into place. But we absolutely shouldn't work in silos—doing so creates its own problems. When one person holds all the cards, everyone else becomes an opponent in the game. I've spoken with leaders who avoid involving teachers in strategic goals, thinking it's "over their heads," and others who keep strategies hidden to avoid resistance. As a learning leader, you know neither of these approaches is effective. Remember, we're in the people business. We want our teams to be on board with us, eager and willing to move in the same direction.

So, yes, strategy itself is simple.

→ Figure out where you are. **But what if no one wants to acknowledge the problems, needs, or changes to be made?**

→ Figure out where you are going. **But what if no one agrees on the destination or can't figure out where to start because they are confused?**

→ Create a plan to get there. **But what if no one wants to be held accountable to the results, leaving everyone moving in different directions?**

It's happened to you before, hasn't it? You've experienced being the person that didn't agree with the change your organization was trying to make. You've been in those meetings where staff members go round and round about what the end goal is or where to start. You've been that confused person who just went about your merry way and "did your own thing," like many other colleagues. This begs the question: "*WHY?*" *Why* is there resistance? *Why* is there a slow and repetitive start? Or *why* is there a clear halt to collective movement forward?

Something is almost always missing when a problem goes on existing or a strategic plan fails. It's something that people need and desire.

CLARITY.

Confusion Versus Clarity

Remember the trip my son and I took to the DMV? I had a strategy for getting his learner's permit, but I lacked clarity on several things. I was confused—about which documents we needed, about the check-in process, and about why the whole ordeal was taking so long when I expected it to be quick. My son was just as confused and frustrated, which led to tension between us. We found ourselves bickering over how to solve the issues we were facing and the best way to handle them. I'm sure you can picture the mother-son exchanges and the irritated sighs. Our bickering only added to the confusion and quiet chaos.

Think about schools and staff. The problems abound, and we all come with our own perspectives and mindsets about each of the problems. The discord among people when it comes to what problems to solve and how to solve them can create confusion. But why? I couldn't put it any better than Donald Miller (2017), who wrote, "The human brain is drawn toward *clarity* and away from *confusion*." Now, let me be clear, it's not always a bad thing to be confused. After all, there is productive confusion that can lead to positive growth. But in the case of organizations lacking clarity, people are most likely experiencing unproductive confusion that persists with seemingly no resolution. And this kind of confusion can do a number on us!

The Effects of Unproductive Confusion

Unproductive confusion can create a sense of defeat and frustration. Teachers, unsure of expectations, spend countless hours preparing lessons, only to face shifting priorities. I recall a first-grade teacher, after a year focused on guided reading, expressing dismay when the emphasis suddenly shifted to whole group phonics: "Can we not get good at just one thing before something else is put on our plates?" Her hard work felt wasted, leading to frustration and a sense of defeat. This ongoing confusion drains staff enthusiasm and undermines the stability needed for an effective learning environment.

Unproductive confusion proliferates stagnancy. Think of those teachers or campuses stuck in their ways, hoping for different results. It's not necessarily resistance to change; as Heath & Heath (2010) explain, that what looks like resistance is often a lack of clarity. They also note that what seems like a people problem is often a situation problem, and what appears as laziness is usually exhaustion. When unproductive confusion takes hold, all three are likely present, resulting in stagnation.

Unproductive confusion depletes confidence. In my first year as an instructional specialist, I offered PD on a mini-lesson framework to teachers overwhelmed by a new boxed curriculum. They were told to use it with "fidelity" (yes, the dreaded "f" word), but no one fully understood what that meant. Some teachers ignored the curriculum; others tried to follow it verbatim. Needless to say, no one was aligned in their approach. My goal was to help them overcome the confusion caused by this "fidelity" mandate, but the damage to their confidence was evident. After the PD, many teachers jotted down cautious first steps on sticky notes (see an example below in Figure 2.2), revealing their lingering uncertainty.

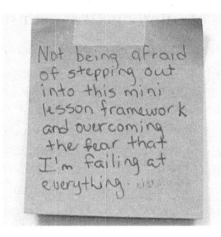

Figure 2.2

Unproductive confusion leads to distrust. As new challenges arise and priorities shift, staff begin to question the competence and intentions of their leaders. Constantly changing goals can erode trust, leading to isolation and a retreat into silos. Trust, once lost, is not easily regained.

Unproductive confusion fosters a culture of quiet chaos and cyclical problems. Without clarity, people seek their own versions of it, often leading to conflicting actions. It's like an anthill that's been disturbed—chaos ensues. But unlike ants that quickly regroup, school staff often lack the clarity and capacity to collaborate effectively, leading to recurring issues.

It's easy to see how a lack of clarity can lead to these negative outcomes. It's also easy to dwell on past failures or current challenges. Many struggle to envision what *could* and *should* be, dismissing it as unattainable. I've heard comments like, "We don't live in a perfect world..." or "That's the ideal, but it's not reality...." These feelings are valid but so very limiting. Thought leaders and ideal situations exist for a reason. If we can't envision potential possibilities, what are we striving toward?

The Effects of Clarity

I'm challenging you, reader, to move forward in this book not living in the world of "Yeah, but ... what if?'" but rather a world of possibilities, "Yeah, and ... Could it be?!" Could it be that we are able to provide clarity to our people? Could it be that creating clarity becomes a habit for us as instructional leaders? If we lean into the definition of clarity provided by the gurus at The Happiness Index (2024), we might just stand to see the positive effects of CLARITY as it multiplies our people: *"Clarity is the ability to think without distraction and to concentrate on relevant information and tasks. It is an essential driver of productivity ..."*

Clarity breeds confidence. In a conference room with twelve teachers, laptops, notebooks, and a whiteboard, I facilitated a backward design process for planning reading units. The process was unfamiliar to them, and the teachers approached the meeting with hesitation, their slouched body language and uncertain glances revealing their lack of confidence.

However, as clarity emerged during the meeting, the atmosphere shifted. Months later, these same teachers gathered again, this time engaged and eager, with pens ready and confidence in their approach. Clarity had transformed their mindset.

When provided with clarity, fear may linger, but it no longer paralyzes. Educators, often pulled in multiple directions, can lose confidence. Yet, with clarity, even one small matter can be tackled with confidence, leading to greater autonomy.

Clarity precedes capacity. Daniel Pink (2011) writes: "The most deeply motivated people ... hitch their desires to a cause larger than themselves" (131) This truth is echoed by thought leaders like Simon Sinek, Andy Stanley, and John Maxwell. It's ingrained in our human nature, as evidenced by Maslow's hierarchy of needs. We all desire to belong. Without belonging, we feel purposeless, and without purpose—anchored in clarity—motivation wanes, leading to a diminished capacity to act.

Clarity fosters collective efficacy. Collective efficacy—a term often tossed around as a buzzword—can feel abstract and unattainable. What does it really mean? How do we know when we've achieved it? While the concept is commonly understood as a group's belief in their collective power to achieve more together, it's not easily seen or felt. Too often, it remains an idea, noble in theory but lacking in action.

So, I want to take the idea of collective efficacy to a new level and encourage you to think about it in a different light. What if collective efficacy meant that our people worked collective toward a common goal *EVEN IF*? *Even if* things get bumpy, we are clear about where we are headed and how we are going to get there. *Even if* we feel a little resistant, we know that we are here to contribute and give back. *Even if* we experience some uncertainty and ask questions, we have clarity around the vision and goals. I'd like to say that collective efficacy is dependent upon clarity, and we'll know we've reached collective efficacy when our people join together to work toward something bigger than themselves, *EVEN IF*.

The Complexity of Clarity

If, as Donald Miller (2017) suggests, the human brain is naturally drawn to clarity, and we can clearly see the positive impact of clarity, then why is it so rarely provided by instructional leaders? And when it is attempted, why is it often poorly executed? There are a couple of reasons for this. First, we live in a complex world, filled with complex people facing complex situations. Working with such complexity is inherently challenging. Second, creating clarity is a leadership skill that is seldom considered, practiced, or mastered.

One of my all-time favorite shows is *The Office*. In the show, the boss, Michael Scott, has a strong aversion to the human resources director, Toby. At one point, Michael, with a foul glare, rhetorically asks Toby, "Why are you the way that you are?" You might have a few of those people in your life. The answer isn't simple, of course. We are who we are because of our experiences, personalities, upbringing, environments, and relationships. Our identity is tied up in all these things and more. And we can't easily separate from that identity, even if we wanted to. As instructional leaders, we are fundamentally in the business of change management. On the surface, we're trying to change actions and behaviors. But at a deeper level, we're working to change mindsets, philosophies, and pedagogy. And we're doing this with complex people who hold tightly to their identities.

Now, when was the last time someone taught you how to create clarity as a leader? Was it part of your leadership training? For that matter, did you receive any leadership training at all? All too often, the path to leadership in schools looks something like this: a classroom teacher excels as a master teacher; that teacher is then sought after for instructional coaching or assistant principal roles; this master teacher turned instructional leader suddenly finds herself in a lonely position—equipped with great classroom practices but lacking the skills to manage adults. Schools, perhaps more than any other organization, fail to cultivate reflective leaders. Creating clarity is not just about being a good communicator, as this book will reveal. It's about developing leadership habits that foster a culture of clarity—one where both leaders and stakeholders strive to align strategy with clarity, enabling them to move forward together.

Strategy and Clarity: Navigating the Quadrants for Success

The difference between strategy and clarity is not always stark. In fact, without investigation, the two can seem relatively similar. It's analogous with the age-old math rule: a square is a rectangle, but a rectangle is not always a square. Strategy can be a series of steps or actions that belong solely to the strategist, the ideator, the inventor. And clarity can belong to the strategist as well. However, while strategy can exist without clarity, clarity cannot exist without strategy.

Remember back in Chapter 1, I referenced Kanold's (2011) PLC Energy Quadrants. If we consider clarity and strategy in a similar way, we might notice similar effects on our culture, as can be seen in the Clarity-Strategy Quadrant below (Figure 2.3).

Clarity-Strategy Quadrant

Maximum Clarity

VOID

CALM
- high engagement
- perseverance
- authentic collaboration
- collective efficacy

Limited Strategy ←————————————→ Ample Strategy

CHAOS
- disengagement
- competition
- resentment
- disinterest

QUIET CHAOS
- limited engagement
- faux collaboration
- stagnant
- indifference

Limited Clarity

Figure 2.3

Quadrant I is labeled as *VOID* because without a strategy, there is nothing about which to be clear. Go ahead, think of what clarity can be brought to if strategy doesn't first exist. Generally speaking, most instructional leaders have at the least limited strategy. A job wouldn't exist for them, otherwise. Which leads us to Quadrant II, where limited strategy is met with limited clarity. In this situation, not only will an internal chaos be experienced, but an external chaos will also exist— disengaged team members who compete instead of collaborate and become disinterested in their work, leading to frustration and resentment.

Even ample strategy with limited clarity, as can be seen in Quadrant III, can create quiet chaos. I'd like to allow the words of Natalie Wexler (2019), author of *The Knowledge Gap,* paint you a picture of this quadrant:

"Far too often, teachers are simply told to do things without having the underlying reasons explained– and without enough of an opportunity to explore and investigate these reasons for themselves. (p. 76)"

It's no wonder engagement is limited, teams experience faux collaboration, teachers become stagnant, and a culture of indifference permeates. Even if an abundance of teachers are, as Ron Clark would say, "runners," the longer a team goes without clarity around strategy, the more difficult it becomes for them to want to engage and be part of the change.

But if we can pair ample strategy with maximum clarity, then not only will we notice higher engagement and authentic collaboration, but we also will see teams persevering together because they WANT to (yes, *even if* things get sticky and muddled). Therein lies (here's *that* term again) collective efficacy. There is no doubt you want this kind of confidence and commitment to flood your campus or district. **But, as with anything worthwhile, it takes more than just differentiating between strategy and clarity.** It takes more than defining those terms. It takes intentional steps, and THAT is exactly what you'll learn about in this book!

CHAPTER 3

The Clarity Cycle Framework

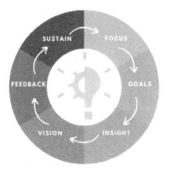

Why the Clarity Cycle Framework

I've got a bit of a funny pride thing when it comes to using my GPS. I always look at the final destination and the step-by-step directions to get there, but you'll never catch me with the voice turned on to tell me each turn. Instead, I keep it on silent, preferring to glance at the big picture of the map and the road ahead. There are two kinds of people when it comes to directions: those who trust Siri or Alexa to lead them one step at a time—no need for the full map, just the next turn—and those who want the whole route laid out so they can choose how to navigate.

In leadership, the same question can arise: do you focus on the big picture or the specific steps? In the introduction, I shared an aspiring leader's story and her BIG question: "How do you get everyone on the same page?" It's a daunting task for sure. Even if you can see the big picture, figuring out the best path—and even the first step—can feel impossible. Or maybe you're skilled at mapping steps, but the big picture seems just out of reach.

This kind of forward movement is COMPLEX. The Clarity Cycle Framework is my attempt to simplify what's complex. This isn't a thick book destined to gather dust on a shelf, nor is it a rigid protocol or a collection of "nice-in-theory" ideas. Right this moment, I'm sitting in a breakout session at a conference and the presenter is sharing steps to school turnaround. There are charts, and tables, and unpacking of every single standard, and using a scripted curriculum, and so on. It sounds great in theory, when you have unlimited time and resources. But we all know that's not the case.

While the Clarity Cycle Framework is not a thick book of rigid protocols, it's not a "one-and-done," either. The Clarity Cycle Framework is practical, actionable, and purposefully cyclical. It's designed to build habits and establish different ways of thinking about leadership, making it sustainable.

I'm confident that the Clarity Cycle Framework can significantly impact a school's culture and, ultimately, student success—but only if you act on it.

And, of course, I can't reference the importance of action without giving a nod to John Hattie's work. What would an educational leadership book be without his research? If you aren't familiar with Hattie's Visible Learning research (2008), take a moment to check out the Visible Learning MetaX resources from Corwin. As Hattie (2023) points out in *Visible Learning: The Sequel*, our challenge is "how to move beyond claiming what works to what works best" (p. 3). His research sheds light on what most impacts student learning and, just as crucially, what has a negative effect.

This research underscores the content of this book. When something has the power to accelerate or positively impact student learning, it has to be acted upon—and done so effectively. That's where YOU come in, as the learning leader. If you can put into practice what you learn here, you'll find that the Clarity Cycle Framework aligns with many of Hattie's (2008) highest-impact influences. In

Figure 3.1, you'll find a few key influences, along with their effect sizes, and see how each connects to this framework.

Influence	Effect Size	Connection
Collective Teacher Efficacy	1.34	When teams are aligned toward a shared vision or goal, they develop a collective belief in their ability to positively impact student outcomes.
Teacher Estimates of Achievement	1.29	With clear direction on where they're headed and an understanding of how to get there—along with targeted, effective feedback—teams make more accurate judgments that drive impactful instruction.
Teacher Credibility	1.09	As we've seen, clarity breeds confidence, which builds capacity. With greater confidence and capability, teachers' credibility with students and peers naturally increases.
Teacher Clarity	0.85	When a leader provides clarity at the campus level, it enables teachers to deliver clearer, more effective instruction for student learning.

Figure 3.1

Developing Learning Leaders

To clarify, the term "learning leader" in this book refers to someone who leads with the intent to continuously learn. A learning leader expects their team members to be continuous learners as well.

You are an example of a learning leader simply by reading this book—and might I just pause to commend you for being a learning leader!

So often people are groomed for certain leadership positions, but the grooming focuses solely on surface-level external behaviors or traits, or it attempts to replicate the current holder of the position. However, we very rarely see the *right* people being "groomed," and we very rarely see the right approach to grooming. In fact, if a leader is being built up as someone to be reflective, develop strategy, and create clarity then we shouldn't call it grooming at all. The truth of the matter is that because people are groomed for these positions, instead of developed, they never go through the processes that make them a leader versus a manager (which we'll dive into here in just a moment).

A learning leader also puts into practice what they learn so that the *potential* for impact becomes a reality. They are not someone who has simply been groomed for a leadership position, but rather one who has gone through habit building processes that give them the skills to bring clarity to their strategy.

Impacting the Learning Community

My kids have grown up with a chore chart. It wasn't until they were teenagers that I finally figured out the best way to clarify those chores. For one of my kids, cleaning was a painstaking process. Aside from the obvious resistance most kids have to chores, each of us had our own version of "clean." For one child, "clean" meant the floor was visible and everything else was stuffed into a closet. Over the years, we've developed a scale of "cleanness" at our house: Daddy-clean (where you might not notice a difference), Momma-clean (it appears clean, with a few key criteria met, and I'll inspect it), and Nana-clean (it's as spotless as a five-star hotel). Rarely does anyone, myself included, get close to Nana-clean.

My point in sharing this is not to compare adults to children. Rather, it's about showing how something as universal as "clean" can actually be quite complex. Without shared understanding and clear criteria, we're left with a kind of quiet chaos we're always trying to sort out. How often do we throw around terms in schools that mean different things to different people? Consider "fidelity"—my definition of fidelity might look very different from yours based on our backgrounds alone. Then there are "norms," "PLCs," "intervention," "guided reading," "scope and sequence," and the list goes on. My colleague and I even recorded a podcast episode about all this jargon! You can check it out using the QR code below.

Catching Up with Casey Show Podcast Episode

Before You Begin, DEFINE: Letting Go of Limiting Lingo

At this point, it might seem like I'm saying everything has to be spelled out, and that's just too time-consuming and micromanaging. What I *am* advocating for, though, is that we understand PEOPLE and that we work intentionally to create a culture of clarity. And this is what the Clarity Cycle Framework aims to do. Because truly, people don't only need to see the end destination, they also need to know the steps to get there. More than that, they need to believe they will have a confident set of leaders who will help get them from point A to point B to point C on their journey. This is what impacts culture!

Creating a Culture of Clarity

I once found myself in an office with a principal, tears streaming down her face as she vented with passion, "Can they not see what I'm trying to do for our school?!" She poured her heart and soul into creating a positive, loving, and fun environment, often working nearly 20 hours a day. Yet, despite her relentless efforts, it simply wasn't clicking.

Want to try a little experiment? Head over to any school leadership Facebook group and use the search function to type in one of these three words: climate, culture, or morale. You'll likely uncover a flood of activities, events, do's and don'ts, and complaints from teachers about a toxic culture—often stemming from being held accountable (I use this term loosely here). Nobody wants to be part of a toxic culture. Everyone strives to build spaces where people feel they truly belong. But, as is often the case in education, there are quite a few misconceptions about culture.

I want to clarify what is meant by culture using the direct words of Anthony Muhammad and Luis F. Cruz (2001) in their book, *Time for Change: 4 Essential Skills for Transformational School and District Leaders.*

> *... educators in a healthy school culture believe that all students can excel, and they willingly challenge and change their own practices to meet that end. That is the environment necessary to create the required change that can prepare students for the 21st century's skill-based job market. We argue that an educational leader's inability to create a healthy school culture is the primary reason school performance goes unchanged or declines and the achievement gap remains wide. (p.14)*

Change like this starts with clarity. That's why I'm so passionate about building a *culture* of clarity—so those aforementioned influences from Hattie's (2008) research can actually take root. But be warned: **changing culture is different from changing climate.** In a recent podcast episode (QR code below), Brandon Jones explained that *climate* is like the weather—it fluctuates based on events and situations, both good and bad. We can impact school climate with a "coffee bar" or a "sunshine cart," but those effects are fleeting; climate can shift in an instant.

Catching Up with Casey
Show Podcast Episode

———————————

Beyond the Buzzwords:
Culture versus Climate
with
Brandon Jones

Culture, however, goes deeper. As Muhammad (2019) explains, culture *"refers to addressing the beliefs, values, motivations, habits, and behaviors of the people who work within the organization"* (p.14). We're talking about more than just buy-in here. If we think about the kind of culture we want to cultivate in our organizations, what we actually want our people to do is COMMIT. While the climate fluctuates, I like to think about culture as people committing to the bigger purpose and collective goal EVEN IF—even if they are having a bad day, even if that legislative bill passes, even if it's "Shocktober," the month that never seems to end.

As you might guess, a shift in culture and true commitment has to start with leadership. Here's the thing, though: beliefs, values, motivations, habits, and behaviors won't change if leaders can't hold people accountable without micromanaging. Leaders who struggle to be empathetically assertive will find it hard to sustain accountability. Without these leadership habits, it's easy to swing to one of two extremes—either neglecting accountability altogether or micromanaging. Figure 3.2 shows this target: we're aiming for accountability with autonomy, driven by empathetic assertiveness. Falling outside this target risks passive-aggressive behavior.

Leadership Target Model

Figure 3.2

Exhibit A: Leadership Target Case Study

When I work with schools as a consultant, they often CC me in team emails to keep me in the loop and allow me to offer relevant guidance and support. Below, I've shared one such email, which I'll examine through the lens of the leadership target model (Figure 3.2). My goal isn't to critique the leader—she's a dedicated, growth-minded professional committed to her school's success, which is why she chose to work with me. But to master the craft of clarity, we must carefully consider how our actions impact others at a granular level.

Here's the email in its entirety:

> *Teachers,*
> *After meeting with your team during planning and discussing the expectations for our students in regards to (content area), we have asked our (content area) experts to model what your (content area schedule) should look like. We feel this is a very valuable learning experience that will help you understand how to incorporate your materials and how to structure your time for (content area). I want you to start thinking about what you observe and incorporate this into your daily routine in class. You will observe both (content) experts, so you can see the variations. We have 5 weeks of school left, and students can still make significant gains. As we move forward for next year, this will be something that is non-negotiable, and we will observe you implementing this during your class. I will be sharing a walkthrough form soon that will be utilized next year and will include the components you are observing. Attached is the schedule for observations. We will come to your class and get your students for specials so you can be on time. Please make sure you are not late. Thank you so much for all you do.*

You might wonder what would need adjusting here—it's assertive, sets high expectations, and clearly outlines the next steps. And while that's all true, let's dig deeper and unpack some specifics in this email.

→ *"I want you to start thinking about what you observe and incorporate this into your daily routine in class."*

With five weeks left in the school year, holding teachers to high standards is valuable. However, consider what standards have been established throughout the year. Have these expectations been communicated consistently? Has the "why" behind this initiative been openly discussed with the team, or was it abruptly introduced without clear context?

→ *"After meeting with your team during planning and discussing the expectations for our students in regards to (content area), we have asked our (content) experts to model what your (content area schedule) should look like."*

The term "expert" is used twice in the email. Think about the message this sends to teachers: that they aren't the experts, but others are. This language, likely intended to provide support, can inadvertently undermine teachers' confidence and sense of autonomy. As we explore in the Clarity Cycle Framework, words carry weight.

→ *"As we move forward next year, this will be something that is non-negotiable, and we will observe you implementing this during your class. I will be sharing a walkthrough form soon that will be utilized next year and will include the components you are observing."*

Setting non-negotiables is crucial; however, when these are introduced without clarity or forethought, they risk feeling like micromanagement, stifling teachers' creativity, autonomy, and morale.

Because I often bridge communication between leaders and teachers, I had the opportunity to hear teachers' responses after this email went out. Here are just a few reactions I heard:

- *"Did you know about this email that was sent?"*
- *"Are we doing something wrong?"*

- *"Why are we doing this next week instead of planning it out? They're just springing it on us."*
- *"I do pretty much the same thing as what I observed. I don't know why they took up our conference time for this."*
- *"Another blanket email—why can't they focus on who needs this?"*
- *"It'd be helpful to see people who are actual classroom teachers doing this."*

This email is a prime example of moving between neglect and micromanagement. If we're aiming to build a culture of clarity and land in that balanced space of assertive leadership—where accountability with autonomy thrives—we must actively develop and refine our leadership habits.

Leadership Habits

Yes, this framework was developed as a cycle. It should not be a "one-and-done" activity. Instead, any step in the Clarity Cycle Framework can and should be revisited as a leader seeks to create clarity. Therefore, the Clarity Cycle Framework should be viewed as a set of leadership habits to be cultivated over time. To become a leader who serves as a catalyst for culture change, you'll need to understand when and how to activate these habits while leading your organization.

Here are the six habits you'll work to develop as you read this book and implement the steps of the Clarity Cycle Framework:

1. **The habit of gathering small teams and identifying areas of focus.**

   Going at things alone is a habit too often practiced. I'm going to encourage you to build a habit of strategically forming appropriate teams based on potential areas of focus.

2. **The habit of analyzing areas of focus and developing goals**

   Too often we determine an area of focus and skip imperative work—this is when we might notice false starts. This step will help you practice the habit of purposefully analyzing an area of focus by identifying both strengths and challenges. Then, and only then, will realistic and aligned goals be developed.

3. **The habit of gaining insight from stakeholders**

   Many leaders may listen to stakeholders, but few do it well and with intentionality. Your charge is to practice the art of listening as you implement listening tours. The hope is that you learn to gain perspective and insight that will better inform the goals and critical moves.

4. **The habit of casting vision and scripting critical moves**
   Casting vision is easier said than done. Expect to step outside your comfort zone as you develop the habit of casting vision effectively and sharing action steps toward goals.

5. **The habit of celebrating systematically and providing feedback**
   The purpose of this habit is to find the bright spots and provide feedback along the way to create momentum and build capacity. The hard part about building this habit is that there is a delicate balance between celebrating and toxic positivity, just as there is a delicate balance between productive feedback and feedback that stalls momentum.

6. **The habit of calibrating to sustain**
   And just like that, you'll make it to the final habit of calibrating to sustain, because we're not in this to see things NOT come to fruition! In this final step, we'll practice the art of monitoring, reflecting, and adjusting accordingly to sustain progress.

Bringing Yourself to this Work

Before you dive into the next chapters and learn about each step of the Clarity Cycle Framework, I want to ask you a really important question:

How will you bring yourself to this work so you can be the best FOR your school?

Are you tackling this book solo, or are you reading alongside colleagues? Are you truly committed to implementing the steps of the Clarity Cycle Framework? Who will you reach out to for accountability? I've had the privilege of guiding schools through this framework, and you don't have to navigate this journey alone. If you try to go it alone, you might find yourself stuck on a hamster wheel—going in circles and making little progress because you weren't clear about your ultimate destination (more on that later). You may end up sitting in your office, feeling frustrated and wondering why people aren't fully committing. Consider bringing me on as a consultant to help you and your team move forward with clarity and purpose.

Finally, have PATIENCE! You won't get it right the first time. It may not be beautiful, but that's because it's not a set of ideas that sound good in theory—it's the development of habits put into action. Once these habits are built, there will be no end to what you and your teams can do!

Part 2: The How

CHAPTER 4

Clarity Cycle Step 1: Select an Area of Focus & Form a Team

The first step of the Clarity Cycle Framework is to strategically form a team based on a potential area of focus as identified by formal or informal data. This chapter serves as your launchpad! It will both ground you and prepare you to take off in one solid direction.

Having too many options can leave me completely paralyzed! The past several weeks, I've been thinking about how to celebrate my mom's 70th birthday in an unforgettable way. I considered everything from parties to Amazon gifts to spa treatments, and finally landed on the idea of a memorable mother-daughter trip. But that, of course, led to even more questions: Where could we go that she hadn't already visited? What would be exciting and unique, yet reasonably priced? The options were overwhelming.

My friends and family tried to help by suggesting things like small road trips to nearby cities, cruises to Cozumel, or hiking in the western states. At some point, I had to just stop asking and go with my gut. I know my mom better than almost anyone (save for my dad, and even then, I think I've got him beat sometimes in the "knowing mom" department). And sure enough, I nailed it—a trip to Asheville, North Carolina that included antique shopping, retail shopping, beautiful scenery, and a whole lotta great food!

Are you wondering how this story at all relates to this book and your situation?

Before you can make any forward movement, you have to determine an area of focus—not many, just one. You have to decide what deserves your focus, why it deserves your focus, and how focusing on this one area will impact the climate and culture of your organization. This can be tough because, as you know, there are always SO many things that require our attention. So how do you narrow it down?

Yes, you could ask your colleagues and staff what they think the campus focus should be, but we also need to consider the stories each of us has crafted and how different those stories might be. We all have unique perspectives, beliefs, and opinions shaped by our individual lenses—just like my friends and family had varied views of my mom and her preferences. Think about the simplest conversations you've had with staff. You'll inevitably hear phrases reflecting different viewpoints on what should or shouldn't be done, how things should be approached, or which rules should be implemented. Here are a few phrases I've heard hundreds of times (and, no, that's NOT an exaggeration):

"You know what they SHOULD have done?"

"Why are we doing _____, when we haven't even _____?"

"If I was in that position, I would/ would not ..."

"It would be better if we/ they..."

"It doesn't even make sense to focus on _____. What we need to do is..."

The list really could go on. You're probably thinking of several other similar phrases you've heard. The reason I bring this up is because it's nearly impossible to determine an appropriate area of focus if we're relying on the opinions of so many different stakeholders. As a principal going through the Clarity Cycle once said, "If you involve everyone, there are just too many opinions to synthesize and another initiative will fail." This is not to say that their voices do not matter—because they absolutely do. In Chapter 6, you'll learn about the importance of stakeholders' voices and how to gain insight to inform the path toward collective efficacy around an area of focus.

But with some things, a decision has to be made by those who have taken a birds-eye view of the organization. This person (or group) is considering not just where the organization should be from the beginning to the end of the year, but rather where the organization could be two, three, or ten years down the road. Better yet, they are considering what kind of sustainable impact will be made on students as a result of collective efficacy around a particular area of focus.

You, as the instructional leader or leadership team, know your campus. You know your organization and have been able to see things from a broader perspective. You undoubtedly have a plethora of ideas about what challenges your campus or district faces. It could very well be that the same challenges have presented themselves cyclically over the course of several months or even years. If you are a district level leader or campus administrator you also know what you would like to see happening on campuses that is ultimately best for students. But beware—you may be tempted to choose an area of focus based on your own passions. So, what do we do instead?

I was able to "go with my gut" when I planned this birthday trip for my mom and me. But the truth is, my "gut decision" was actually based on qualitative data from years of various experiences with my mom. While I'm advocating that you make some gut decisions about an area of focus for your campus or teams, your gut decisions should very much be grounded in data.

Let the Data Drive

You've heard it before, and you'll hear it again—data should be a primary driver of our decisions. It will be no different in this book. Data serves as a necessary tool by which we determine a focus, analyze it, gain insight, script critical moves, celebrate systematically, and sustain progress. When we hear the term "data," it tends to conjure up images of charts, tables, and spreadsheets that showcase success percentages on formal summative assessments. I'm charging you to expand your perspective around authentic data that is people-focused.

Remember that we are, after all, working in a people-focused industry. We are so often told not to take data "personally." But is this even possible? Is it even appropriate to encourage people not to take results and data personally? Now, hear me out: this is not to say that data should be taken personally in a way that has us stuck in limiting beliefs, excuses, or fear. Rather, it should be taken personally in a way that has us striving for change and improvement. It should be taken personally for the pure fact that we want more for our students, our teams, our campuses, and our districts. If this is the case, then the data that drives our decisions for improvement must be varied, valid, reliable, and timely.

I can't forgo an opportunity here to insert a quick refresher on two different types of data we should be considering when selecting an area of focus: quantitative and qualitative. Stretch back to your college days and you'll recall that quantitative data is numerical—any data that can be quantified (think percentages, numeric scores, etc.). Qualitative data is not numerical and is typically expressed in words, symbols, or pictures (think surveys, observations, feedback, etc.). See Figure 4.1 for examples of these types of data. Qualitative and quantitative data drive the focus and drive the makeup of the team leading this work.

Quantitative Data	Qualitative Data
Summative assessment scores Standardized assessment scores Interim norm-referenced assessment scores Attendance rates Class average scores Student-to-teacher ratios Percentages of demographics	Observation notes Anecdotal records Stakeholder survey responses Meeting notes Student/ Classroom/ School Artifacts Feedback meeting notes Digital recordings

Figure 4.1

Data Drives the Focus

As instructional leaders doing this important work, you'll need to approach your focus like planning a precise route on a map, not like a squirrel darting in every direction. Just as I had to choose a specific destination for my mother-daughter trip, you must select one clear area of focus for your organization. You may be thinking that it's impossible to narrow down the list because it's ALL so important and deserves attention. With so many potential priorities swirling in your mind, it's natural to feel this way. But remember, if you try to visit every destination on the map, you'll end up going nowhere fast and definitely nowhere significant. The same holds true in this leadership journey—if everything is important, then nothing is important.

What I've discovered in working with instructional leaders is that they often have a strong gut feeling about what needs significant attention. This insight might come from your campus improvement plans, typically packed with quantitative data like test scores or attendance rates. Or maybe it's driven by a vision—something you're eager to see come to life on your campus. This is where data becomes vital. For example, even if you know deep down that student engagement needs serious attention, you've got to ask yourself: What data backs this up as a priority over other pressing needs, like streamlining the curriculum or refining assessment practices?

You're probably already envisioning data in its many forms—organized by campus, by teacher, by student, by gender, by ethnicity, by program—the list is endless. But before you dive headfirst into this sea of information, let's remember that data isn't just numbers and charts; it's stories, observations, and the little details that paint the whole picture. Numbers can tell you how many, but they won't tell you why or how.

Think about the different ways you're already gathering data, sometimes without even realizing it—through walkthroughs, formal observations, faculty meetings, professional development sessions, and, of course, those endless student assessments. Each of these offers a unique lens to view the issues at hand. A quick walkthrough might reveal disengaged students that test scores don't capture. A faculty meeting could uncover frustrations that never make it into the spreadsheets. All of this—whether it's numbers on a page or conversations in a room—drives the focus and helps you zero in on what truly matters. Below (Figure 4.2) are examples of potential areas of focus. This figure will be referenced periodically in upcoming chapters.

Example Areas of Focus
Overabundance of students in Tiers 2 and 3
Attendance rates seem to continue dropping
Standardized Math test scores are consistently low
Low student engagement and motivation
Teachers requesting an abundance of low-quality resources
PLCs seem pointless and ineffective

Figure 4.2

Data Drives the Team

When I first started as a district instructional specialist, I found myself in a literal and figurative silo. I was the first instructional specialist in the district in quite some time, responsible for two campuses—one primary and one elementary—each with 40 to 50 staff members. Yet, despite my role, I was physically disconnected. My office wasn't on either campus I served, nor in the administration building where my supervisor worked. Instead, I was tucked away in a large office at the middle school, sandwiched between the counselors and the "In-School-Suspension" classroom. To say I felt out of place is an understatement—I felt completely disconnected from the very people I was supposed to support.

But like many eager and passionate instructional leaders, I was determined to make an impact. I was ready to be the change catalyst.

The problem was, I saw myself as *the* catalyst for change, operating on my own, with an almost superhero-like belief that I could single-handedly get everyone moving in the same direction. Looking back, I cringe at my self-assured (okay, let's be honest, cocky) attitude. I thought I was the game changer—cue the imaginary megaphone and superhero cape! But reality quickly set in. Sure, I racked up a few small wins and earned plenty of "pats on the back" from my superiors, but the needle on culture, climate, and student learning didn't budge. I was that hamster in a wheel—spinning furiously but going nowhere fast.

Part of the problem was that I had no real team. My supervisor operated in a different universe, and my colleagues were siloed, just like I was. Yes, there were different teams on each campus—administrative teams, leadership teams, grade-level teams, subject-area teams—but they all functioned separately, living in the land of faux collaboration. I longed for a team to call my own, because, let's face it, making change happen alone is impossible.

Eventually, I realized that the key wasn't in being part of a single team, but rather in being part of multiple teams, all united by a singular vision and driven by the right collection of people. This was a game changer. In fact, I believe now that schools should function as a team of teams. General Stanley McChrystal gives this example in his book, Team of Teams: New Rules of Engagement for a Complex World:

> *On a team of teams, every individual does not have to have a relationship with every other individual; instead, the relationships between the constituent teams need to resemble those between individuals on a given team... we need for them all to be bound by a sense of common purpose ... rather than outperforming the other unit. (p. 128)*

If schools could function as a "team of teams," they would truly experience collective efficacy. Even still, a core team is necessary to act as the guiding coalition—a concept borrowed from Solution Tree's PLC work (2012).

To truly harness the power of a guiding coalition, the selection of team members must be driven by data. But what does that mean in practical terms? It means looking beyond titles and seniority and instead focusing on who can effectively approach the work at hand. The data can reveal who has the necessary skills, experiences, and perspectives to contribute meaningfully to the team's goals. For instance, if your data indicates a significant need for improvement in student engagement, it might be wise to include educators who have demonstrated success in that area, as well as those who bring fresh perspectives that challenge the status quo.

But it's not just about finding the right individuals; it's also about avoiding the pitfalls of groupthink. When assembling a team, diversity in thought is crucial. Groupthink occurs when a team is too homogenous, leading to a lack of critical analysis and innovative solutions. Sunstein and Hastie (2015) share about four problems groups might run into that are worth mentioning here, especially as you read on in the next section about actually meeting with this team of individuals:

- The team members may fail to correct one another's errors and, in turn, actually amplify those errors.
- Team members may fall prey to cascade effects as they follow suit with the words or actions of the person who speaks first, even if they may not fully agree with this person's ideas.
- Teams can become polarized, leaning more heavily into their original beliefs or mindsets without challenging their assumptions.
- The team may avoid critical discussions about unshared information by focusing only on shared information, or what everybody knows already.

Data can help ensure that the team includes a mix of voices—those who are outspoken and those who are reflective, those who are veterans and those who are newer to the field. By deliberately selecting team members who represent a range of perspectives and experiences, you can create a dynamic environment where ideas are rigorously researched and refined before being implemented.

The number of people on your team also matters. Too many voices can lead to chaos and indecision, while too few can result in a lack of insight and perspective. Data should guide you in finding that sweet spot, allowing you to build a team that is large enough to be diverse but small enough to remain agile and focused. Additionally, consider how the makeup of this team will impact the broader climate and culture of your organization. A well-chosen team can set the tone for collaboration, inclusion, and a shared commitment to the vision, influencing the entire organization in a positive way. On the other hand, a poorly selected team can reinforce silos and create resistance, undermining the very change you seek to implement.

Data isn't just a tool—it's your compass. It points you in the right direction, keeping you focused on what truly matters and including the people that will help steer the ship. When used wisely, it cuts through the noise, helping you prioritize the work that will make the biggest impact on your campus. Let the data drive your focus and the makeup of your core team, so you can lead with clarity and purpose TOGETHER.

Unite the Team Leading this Work

"Leaders don't build teams so that others can take a menial role and serve them. They don't hire others to do the dirty work or to become errand runners. They look for the best people they can find so that the team is the best it can be." -John C. Maxwell (2005, p. 266)

If you are doing this work as you read this book, I encourage you to pause and form your core team that can go through this work with you. Are you reading this book with your instructional leadership team? Start there for now! Remember, you'll be building these steps as habits and cycling through them not just now, but throughout your career as a leader. You may also decide to read through the book to build a solid understanding and then pick up the workbook to guide you through this process later on.

Once your core team or guiding coalition is in place, setting them up for success is crucial. This means initiating a strategic, intentional, and clear meeting to get everyone on the same page. In my "Meetings that Matter" training for facilitators and leaders, I focus on what to do before, during, and after meetings—one of my favorite professional learning opportunities. I highly recommend this training to help you lead impactful and purposeful meetings. You can learn more about it on my website, www.catchingupwithcasey.com . For now, in this book, I'll cover essential concepts from this training, including clarifying the purpose, building commitment to the work, and collaborating intentionally.

Clarifying the Purpose

I can picture it now—you've identified the area of focus driven by data, assembled your core team, and you're ready to send out the email inviting them to join the work. But hold on a second! This is not the time for a hasty calendar invite titled "Meet about initiative." This meeting requires some thoughtful pre-planning.

As you draft the invitation, keep these key points in mind:
- **Name the Meeting:** Words have power, which means the name of any meeting carries weight and can shape initial thoughts and expectations. Choose a title that reflects the meeting's purpose and resonates with the team. It doesn't have to be overly complex, but it should be intentional.
- **Clarify the Purpose:** Make sure everyone knows why they are being invited. Provide a clear and specific explanation of the meeting's objective without going into excessive detail. Let the team know that this meeting is about collaborating to align people around a common focus.
- **Explain the Team's Purpose:** While everyone can click at the top to see the recipients of the invitation, it would be apropos to reference each individual. While you don't need to explain why each person was chosen—save that for the meeting—make sure they understand the team's purpose and what you hope they will contribute.
- **Share Any Pre-Work:** Outline any preparatory work needed for a productive first meeting. Even if there isn't

any tangible pre-work, let team members know what they should think about or bring along. Suggest questions they might consider and any evidence or information they could gather that will be useful for the discussion.

Here's an example email (Figure 4.3) for reference. Go ahead, copy and paste! You can also hop on over to an AI platform to help you craft an email that works for you and your situation.

To	Person; Person; Person
Cc	Person
Bcc	Person
Subject	Initial Clarity Cycle Team Meeting

Hi [Person 1], [Person 2], and [Person 3],

Recently, I've been focusing on how to create greater clarity for our campus, particularly by analyzing various data points to identify what needs our attention this year. After reviewing the data, I believe that enhancing the quality of our Tier 1 instruction could have a significant impact on our climate, culture, and student achievement.

I'd like to invite you to join a core team dedicated to this focus using the Clarity Cycle Framework. Our initial Data Analysis meeting is scheduled for Sep 3, 2024, at 2:00 PM in the conference room. Don't worry, I'll arrange coverage for responsibilities you might have during that time!

During this meeting, we'll analyze our focus on high-quality Tier 1 instruction and set campus goals. We'll also begin considering how to gather insights from staff, plan key actions to ensure progress, and develop strategies for providing feedback and celebrating staff/student achievements.

Throughout the next several months we will meet periodically to review and sustain our progress.

Please take some time to consider this invitation and let me know if you have any questions or concerns. I'm happy to meet with you individually if you'd like to discuss this further. Kindly respond to this email by the end of the week to let me know your decision.

Excited about the possibilities!

-Instructional Leader

Figure 4.3

When you have responses, you're ready to begin the initial meeting. And, yet again, you will verbally clarify the purpose of the meeting and the work that will be done together to bring clarity to a common focus.

Committing to the Work

If you're anything like me, you have gotten on the bandwagon of working out or eating healthy more times than you can count. I always start off pretty strong— excited, energized, disciplined. But when life gets hectic or a wrench is thrown in the mix, I can easily fall off that bandwagon and into my old habits. You feel me, right? It's not that we're looking for ways to stop eating healthy and NOT workout. But it can be a hard thing to maintain.

It's very much the same with this work. I'll share more about this in later chapters in regard to the Clarity Cycle itself, but it's important to note here as well. Your team that is leading this work with you will be energized and excited in the beginning. Simon Sinek often claims that people are eager to be a part of something that is bigger than themselves. But you inevitably will struggle as time goes on to maintain the significance of this work. When we become laissez-faire, we might as well stop altogether.

During the meeting, after the purpose and journey ahead have been re-clarified, meaningful norms should be set. I have to be really honest here; I cannot count the number of times I have noticed leaders setting norms that are basically a surface-level list of rules and expectations that have no weight. When you are setting norms, then, it can be helpful to ask, "What will we need to keep in mind to commit to this work? How are we committing to this work each time we meet and outside of these meetings as we get into our daily routines? And what are we going to do to ensure we don't lose stamina—that every meeting matters?"

In my "Meetings that Matter" training, a whole two hours can be dedicated to shifting mindsets about norms and understanding how to build commitment around the work at hand. You can see examples of norms below in Figure 4.4. You'll see how they shift based on schools' areas of focus. Remember, the norms should fit the situation, not the other way around.

> **Example Area of Focus: Learning to analyze and utilize data effectively**

1. Challenge past assumptions and "sacred cows."

2. Look ahead to positive action instead of back to what should have or could have happened in the past.

3. Be present with the people and in the conversations and listen actively without interrupting.

4. Respect everyone's time by staying on task and keeping the conversation focused (limit tangents).

5. Ask questions for clarification to help avoid making assumptions.

6. Separate your own personal feelings from what's best for students/ the district.

> **Example Area of Focus: Reflecting on teaching practices in PLCs**

1. Continuously practice reframing negative mindsets.

2. Don't duck the hard conversations! Practice perception checking to avoid "group think."

3. Show up ready to make these meetings matter. We will get out what we put in.

4. Pause to gain perspective before responding: "How does this affect our staff, students, community, etc?"

Figure 4.4

What's Holding You Back?

What's holding you back? Are you still feeling that twinge of fear about what lies ahead? Maybe it's the uncertainty that's making you hesitate—the not-knowing exactly how things will turn out or whether people will actually get on board with the plan. It's natural to worry, especially when you're taking a leap into something new and uncharted. I felt the same way planning that trip for my mom— wondering if I'd picked the right destination or if she'd truly enjoy it. But if I had waited for the perfect plan to magically fall into place, we might have missed out on an unforgettable experience. Just like that trip, if you're waiting for everything to feel perfectly safe and certain before you move forward, you might never take that step.

And what about the team? Are you second-guessing your choices, wondering if you've picked the right people for the job? Remember, no team is perfect from the start—just as no trip is flawless from the moment you start planning. It's the work you do together, the trust you build, and the clarity you create that will make the team strong. So, embrace the discomfort, push through the doubt, and know that the fear of the unknown is often just a sign that you're on the edge of something truly important. Don't let it hold you back.

Resources to Develop the Habit of Selecting an Area of Focus and Forming a Team

AREA OF FOCUS & TEAM FORMATION

Potential Areas of Focus:	Quantitative Data:	Qualitative Data:
•	•	•
•	•	•
•	•	•
•	•	•

Potential Team Members to Lead this Work:
-
-
-
-
-
-

Potential Contributions:
-
-
-
-
-
-

Casey Watts

COACHING & CONSULTING

CHAPTER 5

Clarity Cycle Step 2: Analyze the Area of Focus to Determine Goals

Identify how a lack of clarity may be impeding educator capacity related to the area of focus and determine possible goals. The second step of the Clarity Cycle Framework is to analyze the area of focus that you've chosen and are ready to bring a team around. This chapter takes this concept from the macro level to the micro level, making it approachable and meaningful.

Would you call yourself a "just go for it and figure it out as you go" kind of person, or more of a "let's analyze every possible outcome" type? I'm usually in the first camp—and sometimes, that lands me in ... interesting situations. Like the time I decided to get to my hotel outside Atlanta as frugally as possible. I was headed to a leadership retreat on the outskirts of the city. Determined to avoid spending a dime more than necessary, I tackled Atlanta's public transportation. The problem? I grew up in a very rural area. Buses, trains, codes, routes—these weren't exactly in my skill set. But off I went, hauling a suitcase and a backpack, hopping from train to bus, and bus to bus. At one point, I missed my stop and overshot my destination by a good bit. Long story short, I found myself walking nearly two miles in the rain. Had I taken the time to better analyze my options, I might have avoided some awkward—and damp—moments.

The truth is, both "think later" types and over-analyzers come with their own set of pros and cons. Jumping in without the right analysis often leads to another failed initiative, while overanalyzing can hold us back from starting or lead us to an approach that lacks impact. We also have to consider that, because no two brains are wired the same, every team member will come at this analytical work with different perspectives and perceptions. This is wonderful, isn't it? But rarely do we actually embrace this truth. Instead, our instincts and habits set in and we spit out thoughts and solutions that we believe the masses *should* hold. Again, this is why the construction of your team is so important.

Not only does the makeup of the team matter, the ways in which the team goes about analyzing data does, too! If teams try to analyze an area of focus without a structured protocol, they rarely land on meaningful goals. What we're aiming for is that happy medium, and we can only get there with a proven structure. In this chapter, I'll introduce a simple structure for analyzing the area of focus. Within this structure, we'll implement protocols and processes to help achieve that balance.

Structure for Analyzing Data or, in this case, the Area of Focus
- Start with Strengths
- Identify Challenges
- Prioritize Goals
- Consider Distractors

Let's take a look at each part of this structure and the processes within to analyze the area of focus effectively and with clarity.

Start with Strengths

How often have you spread out data and jumped straight to what needs improvement? We've all been there. Our brains are naturally wired to focus on the negative—this is called negativity bias. Negativity bias makes us not only notice the negative faster but also dwell on it longer. Cacioppo et al. (2014) explain, "The evolutionary perspective suggests that this tendency to dwell on the negative more than the positive is simply one way the brain tries to keep us safe" (p. 309). In data analysis, our sense of "safety" often comes from improving scores, teaching practices, behavior, attendance, and more. I could go on about the psychology behind "safety" in that list, but let's save that for a coffee chat.

Too often, we brush right past the positives, almost as if they don't exist at all. The thing is, when we only focus on what needs improvement, we unintentionally create that quiet chaos I mentioned back in the first chapter—a constant churn of "not enough." While identifying areas for improvement is crucial for growth, true progress will only happen if we first take time to acknowledge strengths. These areas of strength aren't just feel-good highlights; they're the wellspring of our hope and motivation, fueling us forward. They are what we'll lean on to build and sustain momentum; something we'll revisit when we begin casting vision and scripting critical moves.

Identify Key Wins

It's interesting how, when we're so focused on a problem, it can feel nearly impossible to shift our mindset around things that are going right. In fact, typically when I ask about areas of strength related to the area of focus, teams struggle to formulate a response at first. This is not abnormal. It can be, however, a bit uncomfortable and feel like we're going against the grain of our normal processes. This state of disequilibrium is a good thing! It is priming your brain for deep, meaningful work.

In this part of the Clarity Cycle Framework, you'll identify key wins as related to the area of focus. It may cause you to stretch a bit, and that's okay. Think about what the qualitative or quantitative data reveals about strengths regarding the area of focus. Here is what one Los Angeles school mentioned as strengths related to their area of focus (using data to differentiate instruction, promote student growth, and increase student engagement):

- *"Teachers use classroom data individually to support instruction."*
- *"They use push-in resources for struggling students."*

- *"They utilize different modalities for learning (SG instruction, etc.)."*

Figure 5.1 shows other examples of key wins parallel to various areas of focus a school might choose.

Example Areas of Focus (problem)	Example Potential Key Wins
Overabundance of students in tiers 2 and 3	Tier 2 intervention programs are being implemented consistently Tier 3 interventionists meet regularly to collaborate
Absenteeism is causing students to miss chunks of content and affecting attendance rates	Classrooms X, Y, and Z have the highest consistent attendance rates Attendance rates are higher during these times of year (season, semester, etc.)
Standardized Math test scores are consistently low	When we dissect the data, it seems our students consistently excel in problems related to data analysis
Low student engagement and motivation (resulting in increased behavior issues)	Students are most engaged and motivated during science labs These classroom teachers, X, Y, and Z, submit the fewest office referrals Students report enjoying going to the library each week
Teachers requesting an abundance of resources	Teachers are eager to implement things that target essential skills Most teachers share lesson plans and resources

PLCs seem pointless and ineffective	Teams regularly meet and submit an agenda Most teachers share lesson plans and resources Team C is the most productive and efficient team that enjoys PLCs

Figure 5.1

Organize Your Wins

Once you've identified key wins related to your area of focus, taking the time to organize them can be incredibly impactful. The purpose of this step is to shift your mindset toward what's working and to recognize the growth potential within your organization. While optional, organizing these wins now will provide clarity later in the Clarity Cycle Framework, allowing you to revisit and build upon your strengths with greater intention.

Arranging your key wins from most impactful to least impactful creates an opportunity to analyze what makes them effective. This reflection not only highlights successful strategies but also reveals patterns that can be replicated to drive progress. Even a small dose of hope can emerge from understanding your wins, which strengthens your ability to build on them. Without this step, you risk overlooking the deeper factors contributing to success, potentially missing out on opportunities to amplify your impact.

Identify Challenges

This is where it gets exciting! Why? Because this is where the seeds of change are planted. At this stage, teams shift from observing the big picture to digging into the details, analyzing challenges on a micro level. It's important to remember that the craft of clarity is about balancing perspective: zooming out to see the bigger picture—the destination from a bird's-eye view—and then zooming in repeatedly to uncover the navigational twists and turns needed to reach that destination.

Now that we've established the area of focus and identified strengths, it's time to dig into the challenges preventing progress. These are the barriers keeping us from achieving clarity and building capacity. The guiding question here is *why?*

But let's be honest—when we ask *why*, the initial response is often more of a knee-jerk reaction than a thoughtful reflection. Teams tend to jump to conclusions rooted in long-held assumptions, personal experiences, or familiar narratives. For instance, I worked with a team in East Texas whose area of focus was pulled straight from their campus improvement plan: "... all grade levels will demonstrate a 5% growth on end-of-semester benchmark assessments in Math as compared to their mid-year (December) benchmark." Their focus boiled down to improving math test scores.

When we began identifying the challenges contributing to students' math learning deficit, the responses came quickly and sounded all too familiar:

"Students don't know their math facts."

"These kids can't problem-solve anymore."

"The curriculum is too hard/too easy/too (fill-in-the-blank)."

"The test questions are terrible."

You get the idea, right? I hear nearly exactly the same things everywhere I go—and I've been in schools all over the nation! While they feel valid in the moment, they often represent surface-level reactions that keep us from digging deeper. The real challenge is moving beyond these cyclical complaints to uncover the root causes of the problem.

So how do we keep from chasing excuses and start finding productive solutions? We adhere to a protocol—a structured approach that guides us past assumptions and helps uncover actionable insights. This is where the real work begins.

Conduct a Root Cause Analysis Protocol

My family and I use one of those tracking apps that shows where each of us is at any given moment, where our last stop was, and the speeds at which we've traveled (my son lovingly calls it the "stalker app"). Sometimes it's hard to see exactly where someone's pinpoint is located, especially if it's in a densely populated area with many possible venues, like a strip mall. When that happens, I have to zoom in to get a clearer view. Can you picture us pinching the image on our phones to zoom in? The details suddenly come into focus.

That's exactly what we're doing with a root cause analysis protocol. We're zooming in to move beyond answering the "why" question with assumptions or predispositions. There are several root cause or contributing cause analysis protocols—5 Whys, Pareto Charts, Fishbone Diagrams, and more. However, in this book, I'll be sharing the 10-5-5 protocol. It's essentially a variation of the 5 Whys method.

Several campuses have used this protocol as part of their campus improvement planning, and for good reason—it's highly thought-provoking. It works beautifully in the Clarity Cycle Framework as well. Figures 5.2 and 5.3 outline this protocol step by step, divided into two parts to provide detailed descriptions and bring clarity to the process.

10-5-5 Root or Contributing Cause Analysis (Part 1)

10-5-5 Root or Contributing Cause Analysis (PART 1)	
STEP 1	Construct a problem statement that is supported by objective data.
STEP 2	List 10 possible reasons why the problem might be occurring. Then pause and reflect on trends that are emerging.
STEP 3	List 5 MORE possible reasons why the problem might be occurring. Then pause to reflect on any additional patterns noticed.
STEP 4	List 5 MORE possible reasons why the problem might be occurring.

Figure 5.2

Now, let's pause and dive into some logistics. Remember, your team should have set norms at the beginning of the Clarity Cycle Framework. Before diving into any root cause analysis, it's important to revisit those norms to stay grounded in the purpose of this work and the intended outcomes.

Your problem statement is simply your area of focus written as a complete sentence. For example, if we continue with the earlier case study from East Texas, their problem statement might have been: *"Math assessment scores indicate students are struggling to accurately solve multi-step problems."*

As the team moves into Step 2 and begins listing possible reasons the problem could be occurring, you might notice a few things. First, team members may feel it is impossible to list 20 different things! But I assure you, it is far from impossible. For most teams that are committed to this work, once they get going, it's a challenge to actually stop at 20. If team members get stuck, though, encourage them to take an item already listed and expand on it to create other potential reasons.

Second, depending on who is participating in this protocol, you're likely to hear some common phrases that require reframing. Look back at the earlier bulleted list ("Students don't... these kids can't... the curriculum is/ isn't..."). These statements are focused entirely on external factors, which is a fairly common default. After all, it's challenging to be reflective and consider how we, ourselves, might be contributing to the problem. Once your team has listed the first ten potential reasons, it might be helpful to pause and prompt deeper thinking with sentence stems or guiding questions. You could say something like, *"You've given a lot of thought to external factors. What might we be doing—or not doing—as teachers, leaders, or staff that could be contributing to this issue?"*

Third, many of the things being listed may err on the side of opinions versus facts. It is okay for personal perspectives to be discussed here and even make the list. However, if this is happening too frequently, then we run the risk of shifting into groupthink. Encourage the team to consider if the things they are listing are factual or can be backed by data.

These things will allow your team to shift focus inward, creating space for more thoughtful and reflective responses. From there, you'll be ready to move on to listing additional potential contributing factors.

10-5-5 Root or Contributing Cause Analysis (Part 2)

10-5-5 Root or Contributing Cause Analysis (PART 2)	
STEP 5	Analyze the list of 20 possible reasons why the problem might be occurring. Consider what can be directly controlled, what feels outside of your authority, and what can be influenced.
STEP 5A	Highlight what is directly within your control.
STEP 5B	Underline what feels outside of your authority.
STEP 5C	Place an asterisk next to what can be influenced.
STEP 6	Categorize the list of what can be directly controlled into like categories.

Figure 5.3

After all 20 possible reasons why the problem might be occurring are listed, the team will zoom in a bit more to analyze each item. This analysis is conducted through the lens of controllable versus uncontrollable factors. This is often where the best conversations happen—debating what is and isn't within the team's control, considering who truly has the authority to address certain issues, and challenging assumptions about limits of influence.

When I first implemented the Clarity Cycle Framework, I encouraged participants to strike through items they deemed outside their control. However, after hearing a keynote speaker address this practice, I made a subtle but impactful shift. The speaker argued that crossing out items assumed to be uncontrollable can inadvertently create a defeatist mindset, where participants feel, *"Oh well, I can't control it anyway, so what's the point?"*

While I haven't personally observed this to be the case, I decided to modify my approach. Now, instead of striking through items, participants underline the items that **feel** outside their control. This small adjustment invites deeper reflection and conversation while keeping the door open for reevaluation. As discussions progress, team members may highlight, underline, or asterisk an item, only to change their perspective later—and that's not only okay, it's encouraged.

Once this step is complete, it's time to zoom in just a bit more by focusing solely on the items that appear to be within the team's control. Highlighting or pulling these items aside onto a separate chart paper, whiteboard, or digital space can be helpful. At this stage, the team rereads this refined list with an eye toward identifying common categories or themes.

Using a color-coding system, like this school did (see Figures 5.4 and 5.5), can make it easier to synthesize and organize these items.

10-5-5 PROTOCOL NOTE-TAKING SHEET

Area of Focus:

using data to differentiate instruction, promote student growth, and increase student engagement (lack of student engagement/ not collectively using data)

Why we chose this area of focus:

increase collaboration amongst faculty; build collective efficacy around data

Campus Strengths regarding this focus:

teachers use data individually to support instruction

differentiate for students that are struggling (push-in resources, etc)

utilize different modalities for learning (SG instruction, etc.)

Common categories:

- lack of training on how to use data effectively
- unable to organize data properly
- buy-in is hard because they don't know how to use it
- classroom management is a struggle
- lack of understanding about how to move students to the next level/ skill set/ etc.
- education has evolved- have our instructional practices?

training around data analysis
reflection practices
high impact instructional strategies

Contributing Cause Analysis

- time is very limited

- teacher turnover**

- many different schedules across schools/ meetings are hard to schedule

- **lack of training on how to use data effectively**

- **unable to organize data properly**

- **buy-in is hard because they don't know how to use it**

- Overwhelmed by the task**

- students that are outliers (way low/ way high)

- lack of interest in content**

- **classroom management is a struggle**

- effects of technology at home**

- decrease in students' abilities to focus

- difficulty having interpersonal relationships**

- **lack of understanding about how to move students to the next level/ skill set/ etc.**

- student buy-in**

- lack of parent support**

- lack of relevance**

- **education has evolved- have our instructional practices?**

- fear of inadequacy/ judgement**

- we're missing accurate data**

Casey Watts
COACHING & CONSULTING

Figure 5.4

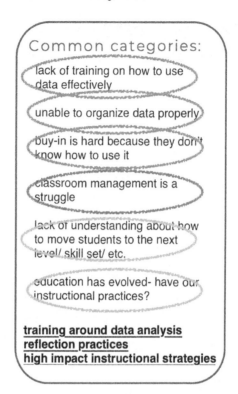

Figure 5.5

By reaching this final step in the root or contributing cause analysis protocol, you've zoomed in to uncover meaningful insights, paving the way to zoom out and craft two to three actionable goals aligned with your overarching focus. The school showcased in Figures 5.4 and 5.5 categorized their list of controllable factors initially into three goals. You can see them in bold print.

Prioritize Goals

The more I think about it, the more I realize this process could apply to tackling a house project, reaching a financial goal, or getting in shape. Too often, we jump into initiatives or goals without truly understanding the problem. We reach for quick fixes and solutions that seem reasonable from one perspective but fail to address the bigger picture. Now, imagine breaking the focus area into smaller, manageable goals after thoroughly understanding the problem. How much better would our chances of making real progress be?

We truly are unpacking and repacking nesting dolls through this approach. Consider Figure 5.6 below. You may have started with the district vision and mission, considered your campus improvement plan, determined and analyzed a single area of focus, and have now broken that down into two or three goals. In the next couple of chapters, we'll take a look at breaking these smaller goals down into even smaller critical moves. For now, we'll stay in the lane of prioritizing goals.

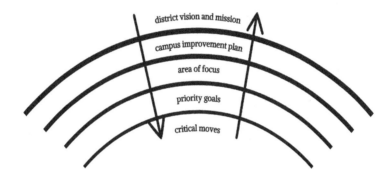

Figure 5.6

Is it Right?

Prioritizing goals goes beyond simply deciding what's important. What's important to you might not align with the priorities of your team or the organization as a whole. To effectively prioritize, consider the guiding question: *"Is it right?"* There are three critical facets to this question:

- Is it the right place?
- Is it the right time?
- Is it under the right circumstances?

As you evaluate your smaller goals, filter them through your district's vision and mission. Ask yourself: *Which goals align with the broader scope of the district's work, and how?* Goals that don't align may need to be adjusted or revised. Next, consider the timing: *Which goals are most appropriate for the current moment?* For example, starting this work mid-year during "Shocktober" might require prioritizing goals that don't overwhelm teachers and staff. Additionally, evaluate the research backing each goal: *Do these goals have evidence-based potential to positively impact student learning?*

Lastly, assess whether the circumstances are conducive to achieving each goal. Are there goals that need to be combined for greater focus? Are there goals that should be released altogether?

As shown in Figure 5.5, the school originally identified three overarching goals. However, after applying these filters and prioritizing, they determined they could streamline their focus into two goals, as illustrated in Figure 5.7.

Focus Area:

using data to differentiate instruction, promote student growth, and increase student engagement (lack of student engagement/ not collectively using data)

Goal Statement and Additional Notes :

With increased training on data analysis, collaboration, and having a reflective approach, we will effectively be able to use the findings to promote student growth.

Goal Statement and Additional Notes:

Provide professional learning around effective, high impact instructional strategies.

Figure 5.7

Consider Distractors

Within the opening paragraphs of De-Implementation: Creating the Space to Focus on What Works, Peter DeWitt (2024) delivers an impeccably relevant quote:

"What we all need is time to focus and cut down on the noise." (p. 10)

To truly make progress, we must commit to making the main thing the main thing. Schools that have engaged in the Clarity Cycle Framework with fidelity and intentionality have experienced remarkable gains. Conversely, those swept up in the whirlwind of distractions struggle to see meaningful outcomes.

On a recent flight to Los Angeles, I watched the latest Twisters movie. While much of the action was wildly unrealistic, its fantastical nature made it thoroughly captivating. In one scene, as the main characters usher pedestrians to safety, some individuals cling stubbornly to their belongings, refusing to let go—even as their lives hang in the balance. Sadly, this scenario mirrors what often happens in schools. People hold tightly to what feels safe and familiar, even if it hinders progress. Despite completing the Clarity Cycle Framework, goals can still fall short if distractors aren't addressed. And sometimes, addressing them isn't enough—they may need to be deliberately de-implemented.

So how do we draw boundaries between our goals and the distractions? Start by revisiting the entire list of factors. Identify which items could serve as potential distractors. Could they require de-implementation? Are there other unseen barriers that might impede progress? Reflect on what leaders or teachers might be holding onto that risks slowing or halting forward movement.

Time to Pump the Brakes!

Congratulations! You have completed your second step and know how to build the habit of analyzing an area of focus and determining goals. You've considered the possible distractors. Now, it's time to pump the brakes! Before you rush forward, take a moment to zoom in one last time (at least for now).

This is the point where you decide how to turn all the hard work you've done into actionable steps. It's time to gain insight from stakeholders so you know exactly the best way to script the critical moves and cast a compelling vision. So, pull over the car, zoom in on the map, and prepare to hit the straight and narrow!

Resources to Develop the Habit of Analyzing an Area of Focus

10-5-5 PROTOCOL

A PROTOCOL FOR IDENTIFYING
CONTRIBUTING CAUSES OF A PROBLEM

- [ ] Construct a problem statement that is supported by objective data.

- [ ] List 10 possible reasons why the problem might be occurring. Then pause and reflect on trends that are emerging.

- [ ] List 5 MORE possible reasons why the problem might be occurring. Then pause to reflect on any additional patterns noticed.

- [ ] List 5 MORE possible reasons why the problem might be occurring.

- [ ] Analyze the list of 20 possible reasons why the problem might be occurring. Consider what can be directly controlled, what feels outside of your authority, and what can be influenced.

   - Highlight what is directly within your controlled.

   - A B C Underline what you feel is outside of your authority.

   - * Place an asterisk next to what can be influenced.

- [ ] Categorize the list of what can be directly controlled into like categories.

Casey Watts
COACHING & CONSULTING

10-5-5 PROTOCOL NOTE-TAKING SHEET

Area of Focus:

Why we chose this
area of focus:

Campus Strengths
regarding this focus:

Common categories:

Contributing Cause Analysis

-
-
-
-
-
-
-
-
-
-

-
-
-
-
-

-
-
-
-
-

Casey Watts
COACHING & CONSULTING

GOAL STATEMENTS & NOTES

District or Campus Vision :

District or Campus Mission :

District or Campus Improvement Plan Considerations:

Focus Area:

Goal Statement and Additional Notes :

Goal Statement and Additional Notes:

Goal Statement and Additional Notes:

Casey Watts
COACHING & CONSULTING

CHAPTER 6

Clarity Cycle Step 3: Gain Insight from Stakeholders

Implement listening tours to gain perspective and insight that will inform the vision and critical moves. This is a critical step in the Clarity Cycle Framework. This step will be revisited frequently and is a powerful leadership habit to build.

Some of the best conversations happen in cars, right? You're stuck in a shared space, with not much else to do, and you usually have the passenger's or driver's full attention. On long drives with my husband, we often dream up big plans for our future or hash out the details of smaller ones. Sometimes, though, one of us springs a fully formed idea on the other, hoping for instant agreement. It doesn't always go as planned—like the time I told my husband, during a long car ride, that I was ready to move out of our "forever home" after just two years of living there. I'd already worked out all the details and, much to my surprise, it didn't quite go as I expected and made for a ... Well, awkward trip.

You and your team have developed a focus and set goals based on what is directly within your control. You've got some momentum now, right?! But just like those car ride conversations, if you've already mapped out every detail without involving others, things might not go over as smoothly as you'd hope. Now it's time to channel that energy into building alignment and commitment across your team. How? By bringing your people into the process through listening tours. In other words, it's time to gain insight from stakeholders. These stakeholders could be a variety of different groups from students, to teachers, to community members. It will highly depend on your area of focus.

Hear me when I say that gaining insight isn't just about gathering opinions. It's about understanding why we seek insight in the first place. The decisions we make as leaders shouldn't rely solely on our perceptions of reality. Instead, they must reflect the perceptions, expertise, and lived experiences of the people we're leading.

> *"Seek first to understand, then be understood."* -Stephen Covey, 1989, The 7 Habits of Highly Effective People: Powerful Lessons in Personal Change

Yes, we might know the problem we want to solve. Yes, our instructional leadership team might already see the big picture of where we're headed. But the how—the exact path we need to take—depends on our people. Without their insight, we're like a rowboat with holes, hoping we'll somehow reach the shore.

Let me be clear—hope can help you float ... but it requires action. Gaining insight is what allows you to create a solid action plan that gets results.

Preparing for the Complexity of Gaining Insight

When my family and I embarked on our National Parks tour, we came across several signs that read, "CAUTION: Enter at Your Own Risk." Naturally, we took the risk anyway because we knew the views would be worth it. Similarly, I feel obligated to put up my own "caution" sign here. Gaining insight is where things get increasingly complex because people are complex. But trust me, the rewards are worth every ounce of effort if you're willing to hone this crucial leadership skill. This part of the Clarity Cycle Framework requires transparency and vulnerability, and those waters aren't always smooth. Let's unpack that.

First, the people providing insight will come with a variety of personalities and perspectives. Navigating these differences can feel daunting. You'll likely ask yourself, "What if they push back? What if they get upset? What if their feedback feels off-topic? What if they feel attacked?" Guess what? These scenarios aren't just possible—they're probable. Believe me, I've experienced them all!

Second, let's not forget about you. You're a complex individual too, with your own personality, perspectives, and emotional investment in the goals you've crafted. Those "what-if" moments will trigger reactions in you—sometimes positive, sometimes not.

To prepare for this work of listening and gaining insight, it's crucial to focus on two key areas: questioning your own assumptions and beliefs, and thoughtfully grounding yourself before you listen.

Check Yourself: Questioning Assumptions and Beliefs

If you're anything like me, you might be eager to jump in and meet with individuals, small groups, or teams to hear their perspectives. For others, this step might feel intimidating. Either way, preparation is key—and that starts with questioning your own assumptions and beliefs about the area of focus, the contributing or root causes, and the goals you've crafted.

Jim Knight (2016) reminds us:

> *Often, people act without even pausing to consider what they believe about how they interact with others. Unfortunately, when people don't think carefully about their beliefs, they can find themselves engaging in far too many unsuccessful conversations. (p. 23)*

The last thing we want is a string of unsuccessful conversations. Taking time to pause and reflect before acting is not something most of us naturally do—it's a learned skill. Before you and your team engage with stakeholders, take a moment to pause and honestly evaluate your own assumptions and beliefs. Consider these questions:

- What are our individual or collective beliefs about the area of focus or the goals we've crafted?

- What do we believe should be true for the benefit of our organization?
- What assumptions are we, individually or collectively, making that might be limiting student, teacher, or organizational capacity?

Let me be frank—this is not the time to pat yourself on the back for thinking you're free of preconceived notions or biases. According to Dr. Mihal Emberton (2021), unconscious bias is a natural part of being human, even for good people like you and me. In an article for the *National Library of Medicine*, she emphasizes that by recognizing and addressing these biases, we can become more effective and impactful in our work.

Sometimes, our assumptions may contradict our beliefs and vice versa. For instance, while I may want to believe that everyone has the potential to grow and change, I might also find myself assuming that certain colleagues will never change. Pulling back the curtain on our unconscious biases—or seeing through the fog they create—can be challenging, but it's essential.

To help get you started, I've included some examples in Figure 6.1 to jog your thinking.

Example Beliefs	Example Assumptions
About Students	**About Students**
All students are capable of learning and achieving growth.	Students who are disengaged don't care about learning.
Every student brings unique strengths, talents, and perspectives to the classroom.	Students' home environments determine their ability to succeed in school.
Students thrive in environments where they feel seen, valued, and supported.	High-performing students don't need as much attention or support.

About Stakeholders	About Stakeholders
Stakeholders want to contribute meaningfully to organizational goals.	Some stakeholders will resist change no matter what.
Everyone has unique expertise and valuable insights to share.	Certain individuals or groups don't understand the "big picture."
People are more likely to support a solution they had a hand in shaping.	Veteran staff are less open to new ideas than newer staff members.
About the Problem or Focus Area	**About the Problem or Focus Area**
The current challenge can be addressed through collective effort.	The current challenge is due to a lack of effort or commitment.
Root causes are complex and require diverse perspectives to uncover.	Teachers aren't meeting expectations because they're not motivated.
Every problem represents an opportunity for growth and innovation.	Students' performance is solely a reflection of their home environment.
About the Goals or Solutions	**About the Goals or Solutions**
Goals should align with the organization's values and mission.	This goal will be universally accepted by the team without question.
Solutions must be sustainable and adaptable to changing circumstances.	A one-size-fits-all solution will address the issue effectively.
Setting clear, measurable objectives improves accountability and progress.	People will immediately see the value in the proposed changes.

About Leadership	About Leadership
Great leaders listen more than they speak.	Leaders must have all the answers to maintain credibility.
Vulnerability and humility are strengths, not weaknesses.	Asking for feedback will be seen as a sign of weakness.
Empowering others to lead creates a stronger team.	Transparency will lead to unnecessary conflict or confusion.

Figure 6.1

As you review these assumptions, take a moment to consider how they might subtly influence your approach to stakeholder engagement. Are these assumptions supporting or hindering your ability to gain meaningful insight? Similarly, reflect on the beliefs listed: Which of them resonate with your leadership style? Are there any that feel aspirational—beliefs you strive to embody more fully? Finally, think about how your current assumptions or actions align with or contradict these beliefs, and what adjustments might help bring your practice closer to your ideals.

Grounding Yourself Before You Listen

My teenage boys are at that stage in life where they're each other's worst enemies and best friends. Some days, they can't even start a conversation without bowing up and immediately going on the defensive. Honestly, I've been guilty of doing the same—putting myself in defense mode before a conversation even begins. You and I both know that when this happens, the conversation rarely ends well or goes anywhere meaningful. All we're focused on are the endless "what ifs" and imaginary scenarios we've created in our minds: *"If they say this, then I'll respond with this..."* or *"I bet they're thinking this..."* or *"They just don't understand, so I'll need to explain it to them...."*

This is why grounding yourself before listening is so incredibly important. One of the most valuable practices for leaders (and humans in general) is the PAUSE. This acronym serves as a purposeful guide for centering yourself before engaging in conversations. You might revisit the PAUSE frequently—before, during, and even after gaining insight from stakeholders. Let's take a moment to pause (pun intended) and break it down:

The PAUSE Method
P: Pause to ponder, pray, or meditate.

Take a second to simply breathe and prepare your mind and body. Reactive listening isn't really listening at all, as we'll unpack later in this chapter. This first step sets the stage for intentional engagement.

A: Accept how you or they might feel or interpret things.

Feelings are natural and often difficult to change, but we *do* have control over how we think about them. Recognize and accept your own emotions, as well as the potential feelings and interpretations of others.

U: Try to understand from other potential perspectives.

The goal here isn't perfection; it's effort. Understanding others' perspectives can be challenging, especially when your passions and beliefs feel at odds with theirs. What matters is the act of attempting to understand—it's an essential step toward building meaningful connections.

S: Separate personal feelings from the situation to become more objective.

This might seem contradictory to "accept feelings," but it's not. Accepting your emotions doesn't mean clinging to them as fact.

Instead, work to separate your feelings from the situation, allowing you to focus on the facts and better understand others' viewpoints.

E: Decide the most appropriate way to engage.

After pausing and grounding yourself, you'll be better prepared to decide how to move forward in conversations. This clarity can make all the difference.

Practicing the PAUSE is an opportunity to build your transparency and vulnerability muscles, both of which are critical for this step of the Clarity Cycle. It's okay to let the people you're engaging with know that you're actively practicing this approach. In fact, it's part of what makes this step so valuable—you're addressing the deeply human side of this work. Susan Scott, author of Fierce Conversations (2004), puts it so well,

"How we enter our conversations is how we emerge from them" (p. 168).

So why not enter with such intention that people will be eager to lean in and engage with us?

Engage and Observe

The time has come—let's dive into a listening tour! If you've been in leadership for any length of time, chances are you've heard of listening tours in some capacity. There's no shortage of information or varied approaches to listening tours available online. In fact, pinpointing the origin or identifying the "founder" of listening tours has proven to be nearly impossible. (Side note: if you ever uncover the history, I'd love to hear about it!) Since there isn't a definitive model, I'll share my own tried-and-true approach to conducting listening tours.

Before diving into the process, let's anchor to a shared understanding. Listening tours are structured opportunities to intentionally hear the thoughts, ideas, concerns, and feelings of stakeholders regarding the area of focus and goals. The purpose is threefold:

- To understand diverse perspectives.
- To identify consistencies and patterns in the feedback.
- To reflect and adjust goals as needed.

This intentional approach prepares you to cast vision and script critical moves—concepts we'll explore in the next chapter. The Listening Tour Cycle graphic in Figure 6.2 illustrates this process.

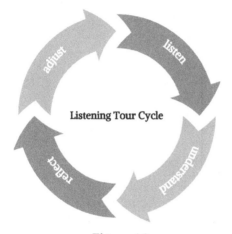

Figure 6.2

Navigating Common Questions

Over time, those implementing the Clarity Cycle Framework have raised logistical questions about listening tours, often tied to one common concern: time.

- *How can we hear from all the stakeholders we want to engage with limited time?*
- *Can a listening tour happen in a faculty meeting with the entire staff present?*
- *What about meeting with teams of teachers instead of individuals?*
- *Could we use anonymous digital surveys, like Google Forms, instead?*

These are valid questions, and none of these approaches are inherently wrong. However, for best results, I encourage prioritizing face-to-face conversations in small groups as the gold standard for listening tours.

Why Face-to-Face Matters

Hosting listening tours in large groups, whole-staff meetings, or via surveys may seem like efficient options, but they limit your ability to truly listen. These methods often miss the subtleties—the tone, body language, and natural flow of dialogue—that reveal more than the words alone.

I'm not suggesting you should never use larger meetings or digital surveys. They have their place in gathering input. But if you cut corners or rely solely on these tools, you risk losing the deeper insights that come from intimate, genuine conversations. When you take the time to engage stakeholders in small settings, you create space for real listening—the kind that builds trust, uncovers nuances, and informs your next steps in a meaningful way.

What we make time for (and what we don't make time for) will show up in the culture of our organization. Prioritize listening tours. The investment is well worth the clarity and connection you'll gain.

Start with Purpose

Introducing a listening tour is more than just setting up meetings—it's about laying a foundation of trust and clarity. To ensure stakeholders feel valued and heard, it's crucial to approach this step with intentionality. Transparency in communication and selecting the right leaders to engage with stakeholders will set the tone for meaningful and productive conversations. In this section, we'll explore how to clearly communicate the purpose of listening tours and why the individuals leading them play a critical role in their success.

Transparency in Communication

It might seem straightforward to announce, "Hey, we're scheduling listening tours." But as leaders, we know the weight that words carry. When the purpose and logistics of listening tours aren't communicated clearly, we risk sending people into quiet chaos. Without clarity, a few stakeholders may get excited, but many are likely to feel skeptical or even uneasy. The goal is to spark an eager curiosity—and we can achieve this by being transparent and intentional in our communication.

Whether you choose to share details during a faculty meeting or through email, it's important to explain three key points: what listening tours are, their purpose, and when they will occur. Don't forget to outline what comes next after the listening tours, so participants understand the bigger picture.

Now, I can imagine you sitting at your computer, hands hovering over the keyboard, typing, deleting, and retyping your message. I've been there, too. The moment you hit send, those words are out there for good, and it's natural to worry about whether your message will be understood as intended. Misunderstandings can happen, even when we think we're being crystal clear. To help you navigate this, take a look at the example email in Figure 6.3. This is a real message sent to teachers in a district when our focus was implementing small-group reading instruction. Notice how the email balances brevity with clarity, ensuring the message is both concise and easy to understand.

You'll notice this email also includes links to videos. We wanted to ensure staff had ample opportunities to hear about and understand listening tours, tailoring their engagement to the level of detail they felt they needed. To achieve this, we used an app called Marco Polo to create Sharecasts—brief video messages shared at the beginning and end of each week. This allowed staff to stay "In-the-Know-On-the-Go" (a name we coined for the Sharecasts). One of these Sharecasts explained listening tours in under three minutes, offering a quick, clear overview. The email served as a formal follow-up to these videos, providing additional details and logistics about the listening tours.

To	Person; Person; Person
Cc	Person
Bcc	Person
Subject	See you soon for Listening Tours!

Hi Second Grade Team!

We are nearing the end of the school year and want to prepare for the year to come in ways that leave you feeling clear, confident, and empowered. Our leadership team has determined an area of focus and two potential goals for next year that we'd like your feedback on. As mentioned in yesterday's announcements, we are setting aside time to implement <u>listening tours</u> *the week of (potential date range). We will meet with your team on (day, time, location).*

During this meeting, we'll share the vision and goals for the year ahead and ask a few questions to help us create a plan for working toward them. Here are some questions you can expect:

Tell us what comes to mind about this vision/ these goals.

How would you define small group reading instruction? What are the different ways you implement them in your classroom?

How could these goals, after being accomplished, help your students/you?

What worries or concerns you regarding these goals?

What does support look like to help you/your team/our campus reach these goals?

If you are curious to learn more about listening tours, click the play button here to see yesterday's announcement! ▶

As confirmation that you read this email, please respond with a norm that you believe will help us have productive conversations!

Figure 6.3

Situate the Listening Tours

When it's time to begin the listening tours, your feelings may vary depending on the team or individual you're meeting with. You might anticipate tense or awkward moments, or you might expect the conversations to be smooth and easy. Either way, avoid making snap judgments and instead focus on setting the stage for an open, responsive environment. How you situate yourself and the meeting space might seem like a minor detail, but it can have a profound impact on the outcomes.

Here are some key questions to consider when preparing for listening tours:

- **Who will conduct the listening tours?** Will it be the principal, a group of administrators, or the leadership team?
- **Where will the listening tours take place?** In teachers' classrooms, the administrator's office, or a conference room?
- **How will the space be arranged?** Will you sit in a circular format, at desks, or in comfortable chairs across from one another?

When working with schools to implement the Clarity Cycle Framework, I often observe listening tours in action to provide feedback as an unbiased third party. A recurring theme I've noticed is how the physical setup of the meeting impacts the tone of the conversation. It's natural to prioritize our own comfort—whether it's sitting behind a desk, grouping with fellow leaders, or positioning ourselves in a way that reinforces hierarchy. But to foster a collaborative "we" environment rather than an "us versus them" dynamic, we must intentionally situate the space to promote openness and connection.

Here's the advice I frequently offer:

- **Limit the number of listeners.** Ideally, this should include individuals who have already established trust with stakeholders. In some cases, this might mean the principal doesn't lead the listening tours—though this is rare, it's worth considering.

- **Choose the right setting.** The space should be comfortable enough to put participants at ease but not so casual that it distracts from the purpose.

- **Aim for a roundtable format.** This arrangement ensures everyone can see and be seen, fostering a sense of shared purpose and value. If a roundtable isn't feasible, arrange seating so participants can still make eye contact and feel included. It's perfectly fine to explain the intent behind these choices to participants.

- **Step out from behind the desk.** For one-on-one tours, especially in an office setting, avoid creating a physical barrier by sitting behind a desk. Opt for side-by-side or face-to-face seating to establish a more equal footing.

Finally, as everyone settles in, take a moment to revisit the norms and purpose of the listening tours with a reassuring and open demeanor. All of this will help set the tone for honest and meaningful conversations.

Ask and You Shall Receive

I've taken you as far as what to do before the meeting, but what about the actual meeting itself? There's still work to be done to ensure the listening tours are as productive and meaningful as possible. In fact, the next two strategies will determine whether you're met with crickets and awkward silences or thoughtful, impactful responses.

The goal is for everyone—both the listeners and stakeholders—to walk away from the listening tours feeling a sense of relief, hope, and even connection. When done well, these conversations can bring clarity and inspire joy, even when the topics are challenging. It all hinges on asking the right questions and truly listening to understand.

Lead with Curiosity

I'm a naturally curious person. One of my Working Geniuses, in fact, is the genius of Wonder. Oddly enough, I don't always lead conversations with curiosity. It wasn't until I read Michael Bungay Stanier's (2020) book, The Coaching Habit: Say Less, Ask More, and Change the Way You Lead Forever, that I realized how often I actually say more and ask less.

Listening tours are a prime opportunity to practice the skill of asking open-ended, perspective-seeking questions. These kinds of questions not only invite deeper insights but also create space for stakeholders to feel valued and truly heard.

To help you level up your listening tours, I've included a list of curated questions at the end of this chapter (see Questions That Level Up). These are designed to explore the "Who," "What," "Why," and "How" behind your area of focus. Some of my personal favorites include:

- What's on your mind about...?
- Who stands to benefit from this?
- Why do you believe this is (or is not) important?

Take time to review these questions and choose those that feel most relevant to your goals. When you approach listening tours with curiosity, you'll be able to listen more intently and uncover insights that might have otherwise gone unnoticed.

Listen to Understand.

The International Listening Association (ILA) (2024) defines active listening as "the process of receiving, constructing meaning, and responding to spoken and/or nonverbal messages." So we can deduct that listening to understand is more than just hearing words—

it's an active, empathetic process that requires intentionality and presence. It's about fully grasping the speaker's message, perspective, and feelings, even when the conversation touches on challenging or emotionally charged topics. And in the education world, individuals are often passionate (that's one word), about topics toward which they feel personally invested. Jim Knight shares in his book, Better Conversations (2016), that the problem is we often don't listen to understand, but rather to respond—especially when we want to justify a stance or set of decisions.

Michael Bungay Stanier (2020) captures this challenge in The Advice Trap:

> *But it turns out that... staying curious a little longer is harder than most of us thought. No matter our good intentions, we love to give advice... As soon as someone starts talking, our plan to be curious goes out the door and our Advice Monster looms out of our subconscious, rubbing its hands and declaring, 'I'm about to add some value to this conversation!' (p.3)*

The temptation to leap into problem-solving, advising, or justifying can be strong during a listening tour, but listening to understand requires us to resist that "Advice Monster" and stay curious longer. It will take practice, but it's important to suspend judgment, set aside assumptions, and focus completely on stakeholders' words, tone, and body language.

Body language, in particular, speaks volumes—sometimes even more than the words being said. Observing non-verbal cues like posture, facial expressions, and gestures can provide insight into unspoken feelings or perspectives. This is exactly why situating the meeting from the get-go is important. Situating the meeting gives us the opportunity to promote healthy conversational body language.

So, what are the practical things we can do to listen to understand?

1. **Take Adequate and Objective Notes**
   You may decide to explain before asking questions that you'll be taking notes. It could be beneficial to share

exactly why you'll be taking notes and what you intend to do with the notes after listening tours. Avoid assigning names to responses or observation data. This ensures the feedback remains neutral and protects the anonymity of those sharing their thoughts. After all, you are not focused on individual responses, but rather considering responses as a whole to note patterns and consistencies in the organization.

2. **Use an Assumption Filter**
    Before forming conclusions, ask yourself: Am I making assumptions based on my own biases or preconceptions? Consider employing perception-checking to clarify intent and meaning rather than jumping to conclusions. I share about perception-checking, a strategy explained by Susan Scott in her book, Fierce Conversations (2002), in a podcast episode that can be found below.

Catching Up with Casey
Show Podcast Episode

Building Confidence in
Crucial Conversations

3   **Be Fully Present**
    The key term here is "FULLY"! I don't know about you, but a personal pet peeve of mine is when people I'm talking to get distracted—distracted by technology, passersby, fidgets, you name it. To be honest, I probably need to work on not letting this peeve me so much. My inner monologue in these situations is, "They really don't care what I have to say—this must not be important to them, and thus, I'm not important to them."

What I'm urging you to do is be fully aware of your presence. This means setting aside distractions, pausing your inner dialogue, and engaging fully with the speaker. Ask clarifying questions when necessary, but always let curiosity lead the way.

When you step into a conversation with empathy and a real curiosity to understand, you're creating a space where people feel truly seen, heard, and valued. It's like saying, "Hey, your voice matters here." And guess what? That kind of connection doesn't just build trust—it sets the stage for collaboration that actually works and problem-solving that sticks. As you move into the next components of the Clarity Cycle Framework, this foundation of trust and understanding will make the entire process smoother, more impactful, and—dare I say it—actually enjoyable.

So, what did you discover?

Picture us sitting together over a cup of coffee to debrief your listening tours. I'd probably be leaning in, hands wrapped around my warm mug, smiling, eyes wide, and with raised eyebrows ask, "So... What's on your mind? What did you discover?" After wrapping up listening tours, I can't stress enough the importance of carving out uninterrupted time to reflect meaningfully on what you've learned.

Reflect Intentionally

Reflection isn't just glancing over notes—it's digging in, looking for consistencies, patterns, and even surprises in the feedback. I won't give you examples because I don't want to steer you away from your own discoveries, but here are some key questions you (or your team) can ask during this time:

- What assumptions did we bring into this process that were inaccurate or unexpected?
- What misconceptions were uncovered?

- What do stakeholders feel confident about or proud of? What strengths can we leverage as we move forward to cast a vision and script critical moves?
- Who are our "runners"—those who are ready to lead the charge? And who might need extra support to get on board?

This is your chance to get clarity—not just about how you're going to get where you're headed, but about the unique dynamics and strengths of your teams.

Taking Action on Reflections

Now you have to take ACTION on your reflections! What you do with these reflections is what really counts. Too often, I've seen leaders either stall out here or make quick decisions that lead to failed initiatives, or worse, back to that quiet chaos we all dread.

This moment is pivotal. Because you've taken the time to really listen, your stakeholders are going to be watching and waiting—curious about what's next, wondering how goals will shift, and what it all means for them.

The data you've gathered will help you do one of three things: fine-tune your existing goals, reprioritize based on what you've learned, or identify a strong starting point for what's ahead. Whatever direction you take, remember that this is where trust and momentum meet. The way you move forward will set the tone for everything that follows.

Resources to Develop the Habit of Gaining Insight from Stakeholders

Gaining Insight "Do's and Don'ts"

Don't...	Do...
...deliver unclear messages.	...be intentional and clear about the purpose and the hopeful outcome.
...do most of the talking.	...listen with your whole self and listen to understand.
...assume you understand or make assumptions about what someone is communicating.	...ask clarifying questions, paraphrase, and check your perception.
...take or make it personal.	...be receptive and objective.
...allow interruptions.	...remain focused and expect full attention.
...run out of time.	...stay on topic and adhere to the agenda.
...cancel the meeting.	...stick with meeting time.

GAINING INSIGHT BRAINSTORMING DOCUMENT

Team's Beliefs about the Goals

Team's Possible Assumptions about the Goals

How can we approach gaining insight from stakeholders? Who will we reach out to? What questions might we ask based on our beliefs and assumptions?

Casey Watts
COACHING & CONSULTING

LISTENING TOUR PLANNING DOCUMENT

Date :

Campus :

Purpose of the Listening Tour(s)/ Feedback Meeting(s) :

Facilitators :

Attendees :

Questions/ Prompts :

Notes :

Casey Watts
COACHING & CONSULTING

QUESTIONS THAT *level up* FEEDBACK MEETINGS

WHAT
- What's on your mind about...?
- What evidence shows long-term benefits for our staff and students?
- What has this looked like for you?
- What is your understanding of this?

WHO
- Who stands to benefit from this?
- Who should be leading this? In what way?
- Who has this/ would this this impact in a positive way/ negative way?
- Who needs to know about this?

WHY
- Why should our school focus on this right now?
- Why is this relevant to our school?
- Why do you believe this is/ is not important?

HOW
- How would this look if implemented well?
- How have you implemented this so far?
- How has this affected you/ your students?
- How should we move forward?

Casey Watts
COACHING & CONSULTING

CHAPTER 7

Clarity Cycle Step 4: Script Critical Moves & Cast Vision

The fourth step of the Clarity Cycle Framework focuses on crafting actionable steps and aligning teams around a shared vision. This chapter will help you bridge the gap between goals and execution, turning intentions into meaningful progress.

If you haven't noticed by now, travel is a recurring theme throughout this book—and for good reason. I can think of no better metaphor for clarity work. Stretch back to the beginning of this book when I shared the story of our family vacation, the Watts National Parks Tour. You might remember my youngest son's endless questions and how they tested every ounce of our patience. But you might also recall the one simple thing that brought clarity and calm to the chaos: a detailed yet flexible written schedule. Essentially, we considered his endless line of questions and thinking and, using that insight, scripted the critical moves.

This is exactly what you'll be doing with your area of focus, goals, and the insight you've gained from stakeholders. You'll zoom out to see the bigger picture—the vision of where everyone is headed—and then zoom in to develop the critical moves that will get everyone there. The listening tours from the last chapter play an essential role in this process. You may have discovered through these tours that the action steps you initially assumed would help achieve the goals might not be as effective as you thought. For example, after one school engaged in listening tours, they realized they couldn't jump straight into learning about high-impact Tier 1 instructional strategies. Instead, they found that teachers lacked a common understanding of a lesson cycle, which meant their actionable steps had to shift. These actionable steps, the ones informed by meaningful insight, are the critical moves.

Even after developing these critical moves, you'll still face the ongoing challenge of casting a vision for the desired destination and the pathway to get there (just like we scripted critical moves for our road trip across the country—we still had to continuously revisit the schedule and cast vision each step of the way). While the terms "vision" and "mission" often get the spotlight in leadership conversations, I've intentionally used "area of focus" and "goals" throughout this book—and I'm sticking with them. Here's why: your area of focus and goals are inherently tied to the broader district or campus vision and mission, but they allow for greater flexibility and adaptability in the work ahead.

Too often, vision and mission statements are dismissed as lofty or unattainable because they are crafted without the foundational work that makes them actionable. By staying grounded in the language of "area of focus" and "goals," you're leaning into clarity and practicality—something your team can rally around as they do the work. This doesn't mean vision and mission lose their importance; instead, they serve as the North Star while your area of focus and goals carve the path forward.

In some schools, leadership teams have decided to consider what this language looks like in strategic plans. You can see examples of this in Figure 7.1.

We are on a mission to... (area of focus)	By... (goals)
Utilize data to differentiate instruction, increase student engagement, and promote student growth	Learning about and implementing data analysis protocols, reflecting on data intentionally, and using data to inform high impact instructional strategies
Increase state reading test scores by at least 5%	Learning about and implementing common Tier 1 instructional strategies
Create high-functioning professional learning communities that collaborate authentically	Engaging in PLC training, adhering to focused agendas, and implementing common formative assessments
Improve teacher and student attendance rates by 7% and notice an eagerness to come to school	Implementing cognitively engaging lessons and focusing on collaborative planning during PLC meetings

Figure 7.1

These may look like "SMART Goals," and in some ways, they are. But I've intentionally avoided that terminology here because I've found that SMART goals often devolve into little more than checklists, completed out of compliance rather than conviction. Too often, they lose the spark that drives meaningful results. While forms and rigid criteria certainly have their place, they can sometimes strip away the passion and purpose that inspire real change.

It's time to take on the role of cartographer and map the journey to success! How exactly will you script the critical moves and cast a vision to bridge gaps, foster commitment, and create sustainable alignment? Read on to find out!

Starting with the End in Mind

When planning a vacation, you likely start by imagining yourself at the destination. Maybe you can see yourself on the beach—feet in the sand, waves crashing to create that unmatched sense of calm, and your favorite people making memories. You might even visualize the restaurants you'll visit or the satisfaction of laying your head on the pillow after a day full of adventure.

Let's apply that same approach to this work. Where is your organization headed on this journey? Can you see it? You might already be thinking about the area of focus and goals or the mission on which you're headed—but have you actually taken a moment to visualize it? As you start with the end in mind, I encourage you and your team to truly picture what it will look like, sound like, and feel like when the goals are achieved. What will be different once your organization gets there? You may even take it a step further and create a vision board of sorts, one way to keep this work top of mind instead of out of mind (something we'll learn about in the next chapter).

Now, think about where your teams and individuals currently stand in relation to that vision. Using the data and insight gained from listening tours, you can begin scripting critical moves that make the change feel manageable. Once those moves are in place, you'll be ready to clearly communicate the destination to stakeholders—and outline exactly how your organization will get there!

Script the Critical Moves

It is here that I'll be heavily leaning into the work of Chip and Dan Heath from their book *Switch: How to Change Things When Change is Hard* (2010). When we script critical moves—or create actionable steps—we are diving straight into the heart of change management. And here's what Heath & Heath say about leading change:

Many leaders pride themselves on setting high-level direction: I'll set the vision and stay out of the details. It's true that a compelling vision is critical. But it's not enough. Big-picture, hands-off leadership isn't likely to work in a change situation, because the hardest part of change—the paralyzing part—is precisely in the details. (p. 53)

It's fascinating, isn't it? As leaders, you may feel you're providing clear direction, yet your people may still feel uncertain or anxious. When this happens, people tend to fall back on the most familiar, default path. It's easier and more comfortable—even when they believe the vision and goals are worthy and necessary.

But remember, a lack of clarity leads to a lack of capacity. To create clarity, your team needs to break down the area of focus and goals into manageable bites. We want to take what feels ambiguous and make it concrete. Or, as my husband always says, "How do you eat an elephant? One bite at a time." So, let's shrink the change and make it doable!

Shrinking the Change

"Shrink the change. Make the change small enough that they can't help but score a victory." (Heath & Heath, 2010, p. 134)

There are many ways to shrink change, depending on your area of focus and goals. What I'm encouraging is that you start with your current strengths. These strengths will serve as foundational starting points that can be leveraged. Progress toward the goals you've set will largely depend on whether your people believe they can actually accomplish what's being asked of them. This belief hinges on their current knowledge and skill levels, past experiences, and the weight of their existing workload.

When we start by leaning into strengths and focusing on one-degree shifts, progress feels possible. As Timothy Kanold (2011) points out, *"To keep your teams at a level of optimal performance, you must achieve the proper balance between their current knowledge and skill level and the level of complexity for the new task actions or challenges"* (p. 138).

Remember back in chapter two when I mentioned starting with strengths as you analyzed the area of focus? So you don't have to flip all the way back, here's how it reads: *"These areas of strength aren't just feel-good highlights; they're the wellspring of our hope and motivation, fueling us forward. They are what we'll lean on to build and sustain momentum, something we'll revisit when we begin casting vision and scripting critical moves."*

Now it's time to revisit those areas of strength you identified earlier. Review them and consider how they fit into the next steps for scripting critical moves. Imagine you're planning that trip to the beach, with a clear picture of what the destination will look like. But before you get there, you need to map out the journey—one turn, one stop at a time. Your critical moves are the smaller, actionable steps that will propel your stakeholders toward the goals and overarching focus.

Start by asking:

- What is the best first next step?
- What about the step after that?

In Figures 7.2 and 7.3, you'll see examples of how schools have successfully scripted critical moves based on their area of focus and goals.

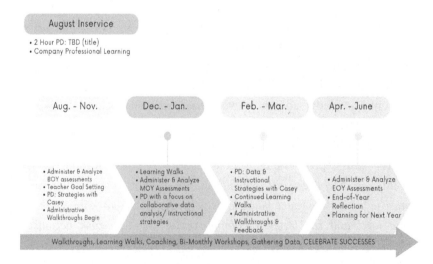

Figure 7.2

This figure outlines the critical moves a campus leadership team developed to work toward their vision of utilizing data to differentiate instruction, increase student engagement, and promote student growth. Their goals included learning about and implementing data analysis protocols, reflecting intentionally on data, and using it to inform high-impact instructional strategies.

To shrink the change, this campus started with professional learning during August inservice, facilitated by a familiar company they had recently worked with—an identified strength. Another strength they built upon was the implementation of benchmark assessments and individual teacher-level data analysis. Their critical move was to shift this practice toward collective, collaborative data analysis.

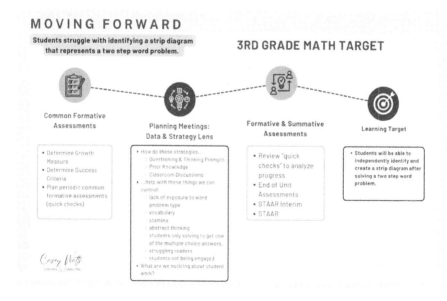

Figure 7.3

This campus focused on improving math scores on state standardized assessments. After vertical alignment meetings to analyze data, they determined that prioritizing critical thinking and multistep word problems would make the greatest impact. While their overall focus and goals remained consistent, each grade level worked to develop specific learning targets tied to solving multistep word problems.

To align efforts, they scripted critical moves by category. For example, every grade level would implement common formative assessments (CFAs) with a detailed list of actions to shrink the change. Every grade level also participated in planning meetings with a focus on data analysis and instructional strategies. These structured steps provided consistency while allowing for some flexibility within grade-level teams.

As you review your own goals and strengths, think about how you can shrink the change for your teams and make success feel attainable. With the foundation laid, it's time to discuss how guardrails can ensure these critical moves stay aligned with the focus and goals.

Guardrails for Scripting Critical Moves and Shrinking the Change

Picture yourself driving on a winding mountain road. There's a breathtaking view of the valley below, but jagged cliffs loom just inches away. The only thing keeping you on the path is a sturdy set of guardrails. These guardrails don't drive the car for you, but they provide the structure and boundaries that ensure you stay on course. In the same way, guardrails for scripting critical moves keep your people focused and aligned, preventing them from swerving into distractions or veering off the path to your goals.

As you script critical moves, it's crucial to ask yourself a few key questions that serve as your team's guardrails. Start with resources: *What do we currently have available, and what's feasible given these resources?* It's tempting to shoot for the stars, but without the fuel to get there, even the most ambitious plans can stall. Consider both the tangible resources—like time, funding, and materials—and the intangible ones, like team capacity and emotional bandwidth.

Next, think about the people who will drive your bus. *Who are the "runners" on your team—the ones who can champion the work and inspire others to stay the course?* These individuals will have a direct impact on your forward movement, so identifying them early is critical. We'll visit this again in the section on vision casting. At the same time, consider who might struggle to keep pace or need additional support and in what way they may need support.

Finally, define the scope of your critical moves. *How many steps are too many? Too few? How will they be communicated?* Too many steps can overwhelm stakeholders and dilute their focus, while too few can leave people unsure of how to proceed. Think of your critical moves like the mile markers on a highway—they should be clear, spaced just right, and serve as tangible indicators of progress. And just like road signs, the way you communicate these moves matters. Ensure your team knows what's coming next, why it's important, and how their efforts contribute to the overall journey. In other words, it's time to cast the vision!

The Vision Curve

"We are drawn to leaders and organizations that are good at communicating what they believe. Their ability to make us feel like we belong, to make us feel special, safe and not alone is part of what gives them the ability to inspire us." -Simon Sinek, Start with Why 2009, p.55

For the Clarity Cycle Framework to create real change, belief is the fuel that gets us moving. You have to believe in the vision, believe in the work it takes to get there, and—this is key—believe that your people have what it takes to make it happen. It's on *you* to motivate and inspire them into action. If people aren't inspired to *move,* we're not going anywhere. The car stays parked—or maybe it rolls a little in neutral, but we're still stuck. If we want to shift into drive and actually move forward, we have to cast vision in a way that carries—where people don't just see it, but feel it enough to take the wheel alongside us.

Casting a vision is one thing, but getting people to *see* it is another. If they can't *conceive* the vision, they'll never be able to *catch* it. And if they can't catch it, they sure won't be able to *carry* it. If the vision can't be carried by someone other than you or your leadership team, the organization is going to stay stuck—spinning its wheels and going nowhere fast.

And *that*, my friend, is when frustration sets in. You and your team, the very people trying to motivate, inspire, and align everyone, start feeling drained, overwhelmed, and burned out. It's not because the work isn't important—it's because the vision hasn't been communicated in a way that others can truly own and run with. That's why I love John Maxwell's (2005) idea of vision being a "team sport."

I've spent years digging into what it really takes to communicate a vision and inspire people to act—and let me tell you, it's not as simple as it sounds. I've learned from some of the best—Andy Stanley, Simon Sinek, Chip and Dan Heath, John Maxwell, and others—and what they've taught me is this: crafting a vision that *sticks* and drives change happens in four clear stages.

In this section, I'm going to explain the four stages of communicating a vision about your area of focus and goals utilizing a model I've coined as the Vision Curve (Figure 7.4).

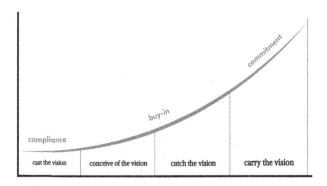

Figure 7.4

Cast the Vision

Let me be clear: while casting vision *becomes* a team effort, it starts with a coach to lead the charge. And that coach is YOU. It's up to you to share the vision, rally people around your area of focus, set clear goals, and outline the critical moves to achieve those goals. Lucky for you, you and your leadership team have already started this work! When you engaged in listening tours, you were casting vision for the area of focus and goals, even if those goals shifted after gaining new insights.

So, what does it *actually* look like to cast vision? More importantly, how do we move from compliance to actual commitment? It's more than just the words you say; you cast vision through your actions, your decisions, and how you show up every single day. Here's what to consider:

1. **Start with Common Language and Definitions**
   Words matter. Period. How will you ensure everyone is speaking the same language and means the same thing when using certain terms? For example, if you're talking about "Tier 1 instruction" or the "lesson cycle," does everyone have the same understanding? We cannot afford to make assumptions about commonly held definitions and beliefs around various terms or ideas. Building this shared language is foundational.

2. **Make Every Conversation Count**
   Whether you're in a faculty meeting, a one-on-one, or having a quick hallway chat, communicate the vision as the *solution* to a problem that must be addressed now. Keep it consistent and compelling. For example, let's say your campus is focused on improving math scores by 5% by developing lesson cycles that intentionally support critical thinking skills when solving multistep word problems. Your elevator pitch might sound something like this: *"You know how we're working to increase our math assessment scores? We believe if we can focus on*

improving critical thinking skills, our scores will improve, but more importantly, our students will thrive for years to come. Have you thought about how you're supporting critical thinking skills when they solve multistep word problems? How can I help?"

Now, I hear you—"Won't people get tired of hearing it? Won't *I* get tired of saying it?" Maybe. But if the vision doesn't roll off your tongue easily, it won't stick for anyone else either.

3. **Filter Decisions Through the Area of Focus and Goals**
   Every decision you make—big or small—should align with your area of focus and goals. Ask yourself:
   - *If I ask this of teachers, how does it support the work we're already doing?*
   - *Does this decision distract from or reinforce our vision?*

   Imagine an opportunity arises to purchase new math software. It's flashy, teachers are excited, and the results look promising. But if it doesn't align with the current goals and vision, is it worth the distraction? Casting vision means saying no to good ideas so you can say yes to the *right* ones.

4. **Hold Yourself Accountable**
   "What did I do today to cast vision for the work we're doing?" This question should become a daily habit for you and your leadership team. Leave a sticky note on your doorframe, set a daily alarm—whatever it takes. Because if you're not intentional about casting vision, it's easy to let it slip through the cracks.

Conceive of the Vision

Our ultimate goal isn't compliance. It isn't even buy-in. It's *commitment*—because commitment is where real change happens. However, people can't catch or carry the vision if they can't *conceive* of it first. To do that, they need to clearly envision what success looks like—not just when the goals are achieved, but at every step along the way. Success must be visualized with each critical move you've laid out. In other words, people need to see what it looks like when a critical move is implemented effectively.

For example, an instructional leader at an independent school in North Georgia faced a significant challenge. The district had set a goal to dramatically increase enrollment over the next two to three years. For this school, where lunch had always been served in classrooms, shifting to a school cafeteria became a necessary step. The leader quickly realized that many of the teachers—who had only ever experienced this *one* school environment—couldn't even imagine how this change would work. To help teachers *conceive* of the vision, they needed to see a functioning cafeteria in action. A clear picture of success had to be painted before anyone could commit to the change. So what did she do? She scheduled a visit to a nearby school!

Now let's bring this closer to home with a critical move from Figure 7.3—implementing *common formative assessments,* or quick checks. To help stakeholders conceive of this vision, it takes more than simply explaining what "common formative assessments" means. People need more than words. They need to *learn* about it, discuss it, and most importantly, *see and experience* examples of what it looks like in action. When, you might ask? Remember—EVERY conversation counts. Whether you've decided to dedicate time to helping people conceive of the vision during PLC meetings, staff meetings, in small groups, or in a flipped format, you absolutely must make it a priority.

Another ideal way to help people conceive of the vision is to clarify non-negotiables or "look-fors" related to your area of focus and goals. Setting these clear parameters not only helps people visualize success, but it also builds confidence that the critical moves are both doable and meaningful.

Catch the Vision

Casting the vision lays the foundation. Conceiving of the vision opens the door. But for the vision to take root and thrive, people have to *catch* it—and that doesn't happen overnight. Albert Bandura's (1997) theory of self-efficacy tells us that "mastery experiences"—successfully navigating challenging tasks—are the most powerful way to build confidence and belief in one's abilities. In other words, people need to experience success firsthand to believe they can achieve the vision. And that takes time, practice, and persistence.

This is where opportunities for action come into play. Your team needs multiple chances to take risks, get their hands dirty, learn through failure, and ultimately succeed. Every small win reinforces their belief in themselves and the work, making the vision feel both real and attainable.

But those opportunities don't create themselves. In the next chapter, we'll talk about the role of systematic celebrations and regular feedback in creating these success moments. These intentional practices ensure your team not only makes progress but sees and *feels* it.

Carry the Vision

When people begin to catch the vision, they will naturally start to *carry* the vision. And one truth about a thriving vision is this: it flourishes in an environment of unity, but it withers in an environment of division. The more vision carriers you have, the stronger your vision becomes. Why? Because every vision carrier becomes a *vision caster*.

We often think of casting vision as something only a "front-and-center" leader does—standing before a room, sharing the vision with a broader audience. Yes, that's part of it. But if vision is a team sport (and I firmly believe it is), then **every conversation, every action,** and every interaction among your people becomes an opportunity to cast the vision.

Here are three key ways to build momentum around the vision by empowering others to carry it:

1. **Identify the Vision Carriers**
   Be intentional about noticing who's carrying the vision forward. Who is demonstrating the critical moves? Who is inspiring others through their example? Vision carriers may emerge in unexpected places—don't overlook them. Pay attention to the teachers, staff, or leaders who are modeling the vision in their everyday work and conversations.

2. **Celebrate the Vision Carriers**
   People need to know that their contributions matter. Take the time to recognize vision carriers publicly and privately. Highlight their efforts in faculty meetings, shout them out in newsletters, or simply write a personal note to say, "I see the way you're living out our vision—and it's making a difference." Celebration isn't fluff; it's fuel. We'll be revisiting this in the next chapter.

3. **Let Them Know *How* They're Casting Vision**
   Be specific. Don't just say, "You're doing a great job!" Instead, connect their actions directly to the area of focus and the goals. For example:
   - *"The way you modeled small group instruction today was such a clear example of what we mean by Tier 1 instruction—it helped your team see what success looks like."*
   - *"Your willingness to try out that formative assessment strategy and share your results with the team brought the vision to life."*

When you have vision carriers, you're multiplying your efforts. Because the more vision carriers you have, the more vision casters you create.

Repeat it Regularly

Keep in mind that casting a vision is constant and it's a habit worth building. Here's what Andy Stanley (2007) says about repeating vision regularly:

> *"To make it stick, you need to find ways to build vision casting into the rhythm of your organization." (p. 34)*

Want to know if you've been successful at casting the vision and repeating it regularly? Ask yourself these questions: *Can people tell me what the area of focus is and what the goals are? Can they explain why? Can they explain how our campus is working to reach those goals?*

If the answer to those questions is a very apparent "Yes!" then hats off to you! If not, that's okay. It's never too late to cast a vision and practice repeating it regularly. And a large part of repeating it regularly exists in how you systematically celebrate and provide feedback!

Resources to Develop the Habit of Scripting Critical Moves & Casting Vision

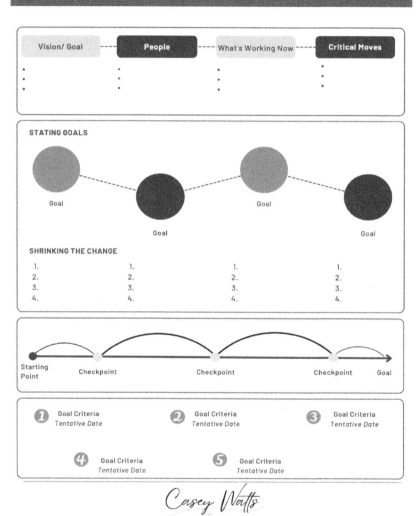

VISION CASTING NOTE-CATCHER

CAST THE VISION	CONCEIVE OF THE VISION
Common language/ definitions:	Areas where examples and models will be necessary: • • • • •
Vision stems:	
What did I do today to cast vision?	
CATCH THE VISION	**CARRY THE VISION**
How will we provide opportunities for mastery experiences? • • • • •	Who can we list as current vision carriers for this work? • • • • •

**Catching Up with Casey
Show Podcast Episode**

How to Get Buy-In For
Your Vision
with
Bethany Rees

**Catching Up with Casey
Show Podcast Episode**

Scripting Critical Moves
with Vision Casting Tools

CHAPTER 8

Clarity Cycle Step 5: Provide Feedback Regularly & Celebrate Systematically

This step ensures the Clarity Cycle Framework remains sustainable and impactful. By identifying and celebrating bright spots, you'll build momentum, maintain accountability, and keep teams aligned and energized. Without consistent feedback and meaningful celebration, the whole framework is at risk of collapsing.

Some people pride themselves on being their child's greatest teacher. I'd like to say I fall into that category, but after attempting to teach my son to drive, I'm not so sure. I've realized I'm too much like my father in these driver's ed situations—quick to offer criticism and stern feedback but not so skilled at providing enough positive reinforcement. It's truly only out of love and wanting my son to be successful, but it's probably not that helpful. I'm sure many of you can relate: teaching a kid to drive can be more than a little stressful. But it's in these high-stress moments that our most practiced habits are on full display.

Working in schools, in any capacity, is stressful. We're so focused on making progress—on top of the barrage of day-to-day tasks—that our gut reaction is often to forge ahead and just check things off the list. It's challenging to remain intentional about feedback and to celebrate authentically. Unfortunately, when things get hectic, these are usually the first things to go. When this happens, the link between vision and accountability breaks, and we often see leaders swinging into micromanagement or neglect, as I mentioned in Chapter 3.

> *"...a leader who simply analyzes needs and makes investments without any **expectation** [emphasis mine] of improvement has only wasted time and resources and will not witness substantive improvement." —Muhammad, Cruz (Time for Change, 2019, p.18)*

That's why we must create systems for providing feedback regularly and celebrating systematically. Developing these two key practices as habits will help us to do the important work that Liz Wiseman (2013) encourages and multiply the intelligence in others on a regular basis. This is how we continue the vision curve and build vision carriers. In this chapter, you'll explore not only the importance of regular feedback and systematic celebration but also what gets in the way and, more importantly, tangible ways to make these things happen.

Providing Feedback Regularly

Is there any doubt that we should provide feedback? Of course not! It's a given, and I'd wager that any school leader we asked would agree that feedback is essential. As John Hattie (1992) highlights, "the most powerful single modification that enhances achievement is feedback." While this is undoubtedly true for student learning, it also holds for professional growth.

You'll notice I use the term "stakeholder" when discussing feedback. That's because everyone contributing to the area of focus and goals deserves regular feedback. When done effectively, feedback builds trust, fosters autonomy, and unites people around the shared vision. The challenge, of course, lies in the logistics of consistently (and effectively) making it happen.

What Gets in the Way and How Do We Make It Happen Anyway?

There's no denying that providing feedback regularly is both important and critical. Yet, there's also no denying the challenges that keep us from doing it consistently—and equitably. Typically, there are three main barriers to regular, effective feedback, and you're likely all too familiar with the first: *lack of time.* It's the most commonly cited obstacle and one we've all wrestled with. The second, *lack of resources,* may feel equally familiar, but I'm hopeful this chapter will leave you with greater confidence in overcoming it. The third barrier, *lack of skill,* is the least acknowledged yet arguably the most important—and it's the one that often holds the key to transformational feedback.

Lack of Time

Yep. It's no secret: what we want more of is the one thing we can't create more of—**time.** Everyone, teachers and leaders alike, wishes they had more of it. But I'll be honest, even if we miraculously gained more hours in the day, week, or year, we'd likely fill them with things that have little impact and still end up wanting more. Would it be beyond nice to have extra time? Absolutely!

The fact is, though, we have exactly the amount of time that currently exists and has *always* existed. So instead of wishing for more, we must decide how to best utilize and prioritize the time we *do* have. Unfortunately, our tendency—especially when time feels tight—is to focus feedback only on those who seem to be in dire need of support or, worse, not provide feedback at all. So how do we circumvent this timeless (pun intended) problem?

First and foremost, just don't— don't let providing feedback take a back seat. I know, it's easier said than done. But to be frank, part of being a leader who makes change happen is sticking to the things you've promised yourself you would prioritize. Providing feedback regularly *has* to be one of those things.

Create a system for providing feedback. Determine: *Who* will provide feedback? *When* will it happen? *How* will it happen? Are administrators giving feedback after walkthroughs? What about leadership team members who are part of this work? Is there space for vision carriers to provide peer feedback? And what does effective feedback actually look like? The less complex the system, the more likely it is to stick. We'll touch more on resources to streamline this later.

Put accountability measures in place. Whether it's having people hold you accountable or relying on virtual tools, accountability helps ensure that feedback becomes a habit and a part of your organization's culture. Here are three simple strategies I've learned from administrators and leadership teams:

1. **Spreadsheet Tracker:** Create a simple, on-the-go spreadsheet to track walkthroughs or instances of feedback. This helps you see who's getting attention and in what ways.

2. **Index Card Shuffle:** Write stakeholders' names on index cards and place them in a box. Each day, delegate someone—a colleague, admin assistant, or even a student—to pull 3–5 cards and place them on your desk. Provide feedback in *some* form to those stakeholders. Once the box is empty, shuffle the cards and start over.

3. **Divide and Conquer:** At the end of each week, sit down with your leadership team to decide which stakeholders each of you will provide feedback to in the coming week.

Lack of Resources

As it turns out, you need fewer resources than you might think to make feedback happen regularly. Often, when we think about providing feedback, we envision formalized processes—lengthy forms filled with "look fors," spaces for observations, and checklists. And those are resources we may feel we lack. While those tools can be helpful, they are not the *only* resources that help us provide feedback.

The two resources you truly need to make feedback effective already exist: stakeholders and an area of focus.

Stakeholders—your teachers and staff—are your most important resource. As Peter DeWitt (2022) explains, stakeholders should be active participants in the feedback process, working on goals that genuinely matter to them.

An area of focus serves as your guiding star. The beauty of working through the *Clarity Cycle Framework* is that by this point, you've identified a clear focus and goals, scripted critical moves, and cast vision. Stakeholders should also have had opportunities to develop their *own* goals within this larger vision.

For example, if a critical move involves implementing cooperative learning structures, stakeholders' individual goals may vary based on their experience with those structures. Some might focus on introducing basic group work protocols, while others might aim to refine or innovate their use of those structures. This clarity eliminates the guesswork: you know *exactly* what to observe and provide feedback on. Walkthroughs, informal visits, PLC meetings, or formal observations all become opportunities to align feedback under the umbrella of campus focus, goals, and personal growth.

So, what does this look like in action? Here are some practical, formal and informal ways to provide feedback that directly connects to your area of focus and campus goals:

- **Formal Methods:** If your team decides to use customized forms to provide feedback aligned with your area of focus and goals, it's crucial to ensure stakeholders are familiar with these tools beforehand. This means dedicating time to explain the purpose of the forms, walking stakeholders through each section, and inviting their feedback or questions. By clarifying expectations and addressing any concerns early on, you build trust and transparency around the feedback process. Additionally, consider giving stakeholders the opportunity to engage with the forms themselves—perhaps by using them for self-assessment or peer observations. This not only demystifies the process but also empowers stakeholders to take ownership of their role in achieving the shared goals.

Google Forms can be customized and automated to send immediate feedback to stakeholders, as can be seen in Figure 8.1. These forms allow for leaders and stakeholders to analyze whole campus consistencies and patterns.

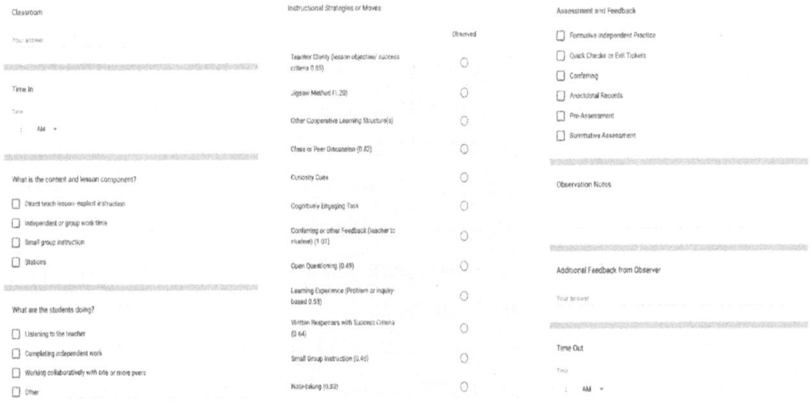

Figure 8.1

Observation templates that target specific "look fors," such as customized walkthrough forms like the one shown in Figure 8.2., can help for less frequent formal observations.

Figure 8.2

- **Informal Methods:** Feedback doesn't always have to be formalized to be impactful. In fact, some of the most meaningful feedback comes from quick, intentional interactions woven into everyday routines. For example, as part of your walkthroughs or casual visits to classrooms, consider leaving handwritten notes with specific, positive feedback tied directly to your campus goals or area of focus or a probing question to promote reflection.

Informal feedback can also happen in brief conversations during transitions, team meetings, or even in the hallway—a quick "I noticed you tried [strategy] today—how do you feel it made a difference?" shows attentiveness and encouragement, as well as encourages reflection. Peer conversations and collaboration can also serve as a form of

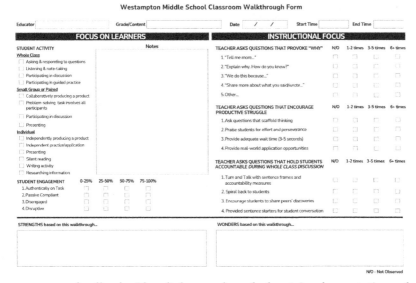

Westampton Middle School Classroom Walkthrough Form

feedback. The dialogue shared about implementation of critical moves anchors stakeholders to the vision and can serve as catalysts for change.

In a northern Alabama elementary school, teachers actively participated in providing feedback through learning walks (Figure 8.3). During these walks, they left sticky notes for their colleagues highlighting specific, positive observations aligned with the established "look fors." These small yet meaningful acts of informal feedback not only reinforced the campus goals but also cultivated a culture of trust, collaboration, and shared growth. The key to this approach is keeping feedback simple, specific, and frequent, ensuring it becomes a seamless and natural part of daily interactions.

Instructional Focus Note-Taking Form	
Classroom Visited:	Classroom Visited:
What components of the lesson cycle are most noticeable? What are the students doing?	
Which cognitive engagement strategies does the teacher use that is similar to what you use?	
What are strategies or tools the teacher uses that is different from what you use?	
What piece of positive feedback are you planning to leave the teacher related to the lesson cycle and/ or cognitive engagement strategies?	
What questions or considerations are you left pondering after this visit?	

Figure 8.3

Lack of Skill

Finally, the third thing we actually DO lack is skill: leaders lack skills for providing feedback and stakeholders lack skills for asking for and receiving feedback. This is not something we are taught as leaders nor is it an inherent skill, so it's worth spending some time on. For feedback to make an impact, leaders need to feel confident giving it, and stakeholders need to feel comfortable asking for and receiving it. Therefore, I'm challenging you to take some time at some point in the school year to explicitly discuss the act of giving and receiving feedback.

Figure 8.4 shows what often happens when leaders attempt to provide feedback and what to do instead.

Feedback Faux Paus	What We Can Commit to Instead
Feedback is outside the area of focus and goals.	Maintain the vision by anchoring feedback to the area of focus and goals. This approach gives feedback purpose and fosters a sense of belonging among stakeholders.
It is vague and broad, making it difficult to act on.	Keep feedback focused and explicit. No one wants to walk away guessing what's next or trying to fill in the blanks.
It is overly positive giving the sense that no growth is necessary.	When feedback is overly positive, it actually depletes trust and mutual respect. Provide truthful feedback always, and in the case that no corrective feedback is needed, provide a challenge or probing reflection question.

It has little room for self-reflection or potential coaching conversations.	Avoid overwhelming stakeholders with too many points, whether strengths or areas of growth. Focus on a definitive next step to ensure progress.
It is provided at the wrong time/ place.	Effective feedback is always timely. However, there is such a thing as "wrong time, wrong place." Monitor when and where you are providing feedback so that the stakeholder can fully attend and respond.
It is overly negative giving the sense of defeat.	While we don't want to be overly positive, we also don't want to sway too far in the other direction. Feedback conversations should result in a sense of purpose and hope.
The purpose and approach to feedback is unclear.	Prefacing your feedback conversation with a structure or guiding stakeholders through the feedback conversation helps them know what to expect and supports follow through (i.e. "I'd like to share something I've noticed that's helping our campus make progress and a way I think you can level up your impact. Is that alright with you?")

Figure 8.4

On the flip side, stakeholders also need to develop the skill of asking for and receiving feedback. Again, this isn't something we're naturally equipped with—it's a skill that must be intentionally cultivated. Let me paint you a picture that might feel all too familiar: You complete a walkthrough and leave a teacher's classroom. A little while later, you cross paths with the teacher. In the middle of a bustling hallway filled with students and colleagues, they ask, "What did you think? How did I do?" It's an awkward moment.

People are eager for feedback, but in their attempt to seek it out, they can unintentionally create challenging situations. What are you supposed to say? There isn't enough time for a full feedback conversation. You don't want to give false or surface-level feedback, but you also don't want to discourage their effort to seek improvement.

This is where setting feedback norms early in the year becomes invaluable—norms for how to ask for feedback, how to give it, and how to receive it. These norms create a shared understanding and make feedback interactions more intentional and productive. Remember, giving and receiving feedback is a skill that needs to be explicitly taught and practiced. For a deeper dive into this topic, check out the podcast episode *The Art of Asking for Feedback*.

**Catching Up with Casey
Show Podcast Episode**

The Art of Asking for
Feedback

Celebrating Systematically

"When you celebrate the right things, you are using the most effective form of vision casting ... [for] what gets celebrated, gets repeated" (Stanley, 2007, p. 40).

What's interesting is that celebrating—whether individually or collectively—is often bypassed. Even though research shows that the brain is more motivated by recognizing how far we've come rather than how far we have to go, we fail to celebrate regularly. And when we *do* celebrate, it often feels awkward and isn't always directly connected to the area of focus or goals. Stakeholders even struggle to determine what and how we should celebrate, likely because it happens so infrequently.

Take this email I sent to a team as an example (Figure 8.5). I used it to recap the area of focus, goals, and critical moves and asked for input on celebrating progress.

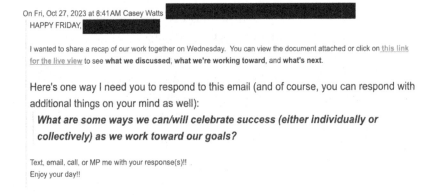

On Fri, Oct 27, 2023 at 8:41 AM Casey Watts ██████████████████████████
HAPPY FRIDAY, ██████████████

I wanted to share a recap of our work together on Wednesday. You can view the document attached or click on this link for the live view to see **what we discussed**, **what we're working toward**, and **what's next**.

Here's one way I need you to respond to this email (and of course, you can respond with additional things on your mind as well):

What are some ways we can/will celebrate success (either individually or collectively) as we work toward our goals?

Text, email, call, or MP me with your response(s)!!
Enjoy your day!!

Figure 8.5

I received a whopping *two* responses, and it was clear the people who did respond were really stretching to figure out what "celebrating progress" even means. But why is this the case?

Educators typically hyperfocus on areas where growth is needed in an attempt to continuously get better. While an eagerness to improve is a desirable trait in stakeholders, it can have reverse effects of defeat, frustration, and even burnout. My belief is that, more often than not, we haven't created a culture of celebration. True celebration requires much more intentionality than a simple "good job." It involves digging beyond surface-level acknowledgments, determining clear criteria for what qualifies as celebration-worthy, and making the process of celebrating systematic.

No More Surface Level Celebration

It is possible to shift to a culture of celebration in a few ways, but again, it takes intentionality and planning. To start, it's essential to move beyond surface-level celebrations. You know the kind—pats on the back, vague verbal praises, chocolate fountains, jeans passes ... the list goes on. These are minor, surface-level acknowledgments. On the flip side, when we hear the term "celebration," we often think of big, event-like activities or overly elaborate public displays. While these things have their place, they don't necessarily make celebrations more meaningful, in-depth, or aligned with our goals.

To truly move beyond surface-level celebrations, we need to start by determining clear criteria for what's worth celebrating. Then, we must decide how to make celebrations systematic—something doable, sustainable, and directly tied to the progress and purpose we're working toward.

Determine Qualifying Criteria

Celebrating progress only feels challenging when we don't have a specific area of focus, targeted goals, or critical moves to guide us to the finish line. The good news is that you've likely already done this work (or, at the very least, you're thinking about it as you read this book). Determining qualifying criteria is as simple as analyzing your critical moves and working with your leadership team to identify what qualifies as progress within those moves.

For example, if a goal is "adhering to focused agendas during PLCs" (see the previous chapter), then a critical move might be creating a common agenda template with teacher leaders. When that critical move is successfully accomplished, it's exactly what should be celebrated.

Preparing to celebrate critical moves and progress toward goals depends on your people. This is where relationships come into play—

knowing your people well matters. Before you can create a system for celebration, you need to consider their preferences for how they like to be celebrated.

Here's how you can start:

- **Survey stakeholders.** Chances are you'll hear crickets at first when you ask something similar to the question in my email earlier. That's okay! It just means you're about to do the meaningful work of creating a culture of celebration. Start with questions like, *"What does progress look like, sound like, and feel like?"* or *"How will we know we've made progress toward our goals?"*

  Once we can envision what progress looks like, it becomes easier to develop criteria for what, how, and when to celebrate. Then, you can follow up with, *"What are ways we can celebrate progress?"*

- **Provide examples of celebrations aligned with the area of focus and goals.** Stakeholders may still struggle to answer those questions, so be prepared to offer examples or probe further with focused, "if/then" questions:
  - *"If you successfully implement (instructional strategy), how would you like to be celebrated? Would you prefer private words of affirmation, public recognition among colleagues, or for someone to observe and offer feedback?"*
  - *"If our campus implements (critical moves) successfully, what might celebrating look like? Would an announcement in our Marco Polo Sharecast work? Could we create a visual display in the hallway? Should we share the success with stakeholders like district leaders, parents, or community members and invite them to observe?"*

Make it Systematic

We can decide to celebrate progress and genuinely believe we'll follow through, but without systemizing celebrations, they won't happen regularly or consistently enough to truly support forward momentum. At best, these celebrations will be sporadic and lack the depth needed to act as a catalyst for meaningful change.

Systemizing celebrations removes the temptation to be lazy or random about recognizing progress. Instead, it allows us to maximize moments of progress and leverage them strategically to achieve our goals. When celebrating becomes systematic, you'll begin to notice a cultural shift—one where people expect to be celebrated authentically, regularly, and equitably. Furthermore, you may even begin to notice the act of celebrating becoming a habit of the people in the organization.

All it takes is deciding *when*, *who*, and *how* to celebrate.

- **When:** As briefly mentioned, the celebration of progress should be something our people can anticipate. It should never come as a surprise or leave them questioning the motives behind it. To create this sense of anticipation, we must establish a habit of authentic celebration. And as with most habits, this requires continuous and structured reminders.

  While you'll naturally look for regular opportunities to celebrate progress, it's equally important to schedule intentional celebration points throughout the year. Use these times to reflect on who has been celebrated, when they were celebrated, and how they were celebrated. From there, create a forward-thinking plan to ensure celebrations remain meaningful.

- **Who:** Celebration should be a collective effort, with everyone participating in recognizing individuals, teams, and the campus as a whole. However, the primary responsibility for ensuring celebrations happen systematically falls on YOU and your leadership team.

Equally important is identifying *who* you are celebrating. As already emphasized, any stakeholder involved in the area of focus and goals must be included in these celebrations. Unfortunately, I've seen far too many crucial stakeholders overlooked—special education teachers, paraprofessionals, custodians, and even some campus instructional leaders.

If clarity is what we're striving to create, it can only be achieved when *everyone* who has the potential to contribute to progress is involved—not just in critical moves and feedback but also in the celebrations that follow.

- **How:** Finally, you'll need to determine how to track progress and keep celebrations top of mind. Will you create a calendar dedicated to celebrating systematically? It could be as simple as setting a recurring calendar reminder every 4-6 weeks with a linked Google Form to monitor progress.

Perhaps you'll institute a "Wins of the Week" Marco Polo Sharecast or newsletter to highlight and celebrate achievements. (You can find out more about using Marco Polo for "Wins of the Week" in the referenced podcast episode.) Notes, letters, or emails also go a long way!

A New Jersey principal implemented a celebration idea she learned at a leadership conference. She asked staff to share the name of the person they tell their proudest moments to. As progress was made, or she noticed stakeholders carrying or casting the vision, she personally called the people on their lists. What a powerful and authentic way to celebrate individuals while simultaneously casting vision, both inside and outside the organization.

Alternatively, you might involve stakeholders during a monthly staff meeting by incorporating a reflective learning structure or protocol specifically designed for celebration. Whatever method you choose, the key is to make it intentional, actionable, and sustainable.

Catching Up with Casey Show on YouTube

Why & How You Should be Utilizing Marco Polo as an Instructional Leader

And One More Important Matter ... YOU!

Don't forget to celebrate yourself and your leadership team for driving this work forward! This is hard work. You're not just checking off tasks; you're working to change mindsets, shift beliefs, and transform the culture of your organization.

If no one has told you yet—what you're doing is exceptional. Fewer than 30% of organizations even begin this type of work, let alone sustain it. And if I haven't said it already, you are exactly the kind of learning leader schools need most right now.

So, take a moment to recognize your own progress. Celebrate the small wins along the way and remind yourself to keep going. This work matters. It will be worth it—not just at the end of the year but for years to come.

Resources to Develop the Habit of Providing Feedback and Celebrating Systematically

CELEBRATION AND FEEDBACK PLANNING DOCUMENT

What does our feedback system look like?

What will we provide feedback on:

When will we provide feedback:

How will we provide feedback?

What does our celebration system look like?

What will we celebrate:

When will we celebrate:

How will we celebrate?

Casey Watts
COACHING & CONSULTING

QUALIFYING CRITERIA & OPTIONS FOR CELEBRATING PROGRESS

Critical Move:

Evidence of Progress:

Critical Move:

Evidence of Progress:

Critical Move:

Evidence of Progress:

OPTIONS FOR CELEBRATION

Casey Watts
COACHING & CONSULTING

WAYS LEADERS HAVE CELEBRATED SYSTEMATICALLY

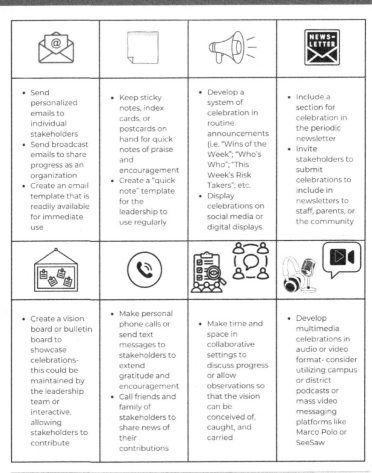

• Send personalized emails to individual stakeholders • Send broadcast emails to share progress as an organization • Create an email template that is readily available for immediate use	• Keep sticky notes, index cards, or postcards on hand for quick notes of praise and encouragement • Create a "quick note" template for the leadership to use regularly	• Develop a system of celebration in routine announcements (i.e. "Wins of the Week"; "Who's Who"; "This Week's Risk Takers"; etc. • Display celebrations on social media or digital displays	• Include a section for celebration in the periodic newsletter • Invite stakeholders to submit celebrations to include in newsletters to staff, parents, or the community
• Create a vision board or bulletin board to showcase celebrations- this could be maintained by the leadership team or interactive, allowing stakeholders to contribute	• Make personal phone calls or send text messages to stakeholders to extend gratitude and encouragement • Call friends and family of stakeholders to share news of their contributions	• Make time and space in collaborative settings to discuss progress or allow observations so that the vision can be conceived of, caught, and carried	• Develop multimedia celebrations in audio or video format- consider utilizing campus or district podcasts or mass video messaging platforms like Marco Polo or SeeSaw

COACHING & CONSULTING

162

CHAPTER 9

Clarity Cycle Step 6: Calibrate & Sustain Progress

This step focuses on monitoring, reflecting, and making intentional adjustments to ensure progress is both meaningful and lasting. By continuously calibrating your efforts, you'll build capacity within your teams and create sustainable momentum that drives ongoing success.

In their book, Switch: How to Change Things When Change Is Hard (2010), Chip and Dan Heath explain how to keep people moving toward a change. They compare the process to becoming a parent—a HUGE shift that requires constant attention and intentional adjustments as you navigate each phase from childhood to adulthood. Change, they remind us, is definitely not a singular event.

Think of the Clarity Cycle as more than just a one-time process— this is about creating leadership habits that ensure your vision becomes a reality. Like any effective habit, consistency is key. Calibration is your chance to assess what's working, refine your strategies, and keep quiet chaos from creeping in. Without regular calibration, your teams may drift into busywork that looks productive but ultimately lacks the alignment needed for true progress.

Remember: visions are refined—they don't change; plans are revised—they rarely stay the same. In other words, your area of focus cannot change. Otherwise, what's this all been for? Calibration allows you to revisit the goals and the critical moves that drive it forward, ensuring they remain relevant without losing their clarity or purpose.

This is also where accountability and autonomy must work in tandem. The leadership target graphic reminds us that sustainable progress isn't about micromanaging every step or letting teams run untethered. Calibration is your opportunity to strike the balance— providing the accountability to keep your goals in sight while granting your teams the autonomy to adapt and innovate within those guardrails. It's a way to lead empathetically and assertively, meeting your people where they are while keeping them aligned with where you're going.

Leadership Target

Figure 9.1

Through calibration, your role is not to change the vision or restart the process—it's to refine and sustain. This step is where clarity becomes resilience as you continuously build and practice the leadership habits outlined in this framework.

Top of Mind or Out of Mind?

When I was a classroom teacher, I often told students to place materials "out of sight, out of mind," usually by moving materials behind them. The goal was simple: eliminate distractions so they could better focus on the lesson at hand. And for the most part, it served our class well.

But in my own day-to-day life, I've noticed that when I put something out of sight, it tends to stay out of mind—sometimes so much so that I forget about it entirely. This isn't the approach we want to take with the Clarity Cycle Framework. Instead of this work fading into the background, we must strive for the exact opposite. Our goal is to keep it not just on our minds but at the very **top of mind.**

Beware—there will always be distractions, competing priorities, or even moments of doubt that tempt you to sidestep or delay the work of creating clarity. It's easy to convince ourselves that certain steps aren't necessary or can wait. But clarity thrives on consistency and intentionality. To avoid derailing your progress, you'll need to establish intentional touchpoints and regularly reflect on the purpose behind this work.

Intentional Touchpoints

It's critical to establish intentional touchpoints where your leadership team can meet regularly to assess progress toward your goals and maintain focus on your overarching vision. Think of these as checkpoints along the journey. They're opportunities to realign, celebrate wins, and troubleshoot challenges before they snowball into bigger issues. But the key here is consistency. When these meetings are scheduled and prioritized on the calendar, they send a clear message: this work matters.

During these touchpoints, revisit the goals and reflect on progress. What's working? What's stalled? And more importantly, what needs adjusting? These meetings aren't just another task to check off the list—they're the glue that keeps your leadership team focused and moving forward with purpose.

Reflecting on Purpose

Reflection isn't just something you do when the work slows down; it's an active part of keeping momentum alive. For every reflection meeting, start with a clearly defined purpose and a well-organized agenda. Use a consistent tracking document or management system to monitor progress. The data you collect should help answer critical questions: Are we staying aligned with our vision? What evidence shows we're making progress? Where are the gaps, and how can we close them?

Reflection meetings should also consider multiple perspectives. What are the insights from your leadership team? What feedback or input are you hearing from staff? Ideally, you want people to be able to see the story of their work unfold over time. This can't happen without some form or forms of documentation. You can find a calibration planning document in the resources at the end of this chapter.

Every Conversation Counts

One of my all-time favorite quotes from Jim Knight (2016) is, *"Our schools are only as good as the conversations within them"* (p. 4). There are few truer words! In his book, *Better Conversations*, Knight dives into the beliefs and habits we must cultivate to have better conversations—those where we position the individuals we're speaking with as genuine dialogical partners.

When you're honing the craft of clarity and striving to sustain progress toward the goals, every conversation truly matters. Adopting the belief that every conversation counts lays the foundation for building trust. That trust, in turn, fosters better conversations, where even the tough, crucial conversations are embraced and lead to productive outcomes. Do I really mean *every* conversation? Absolutely! From those casual, passing chats by the copier to the formal discussions in meetings, every exchange has the potential to move the work forward.

Copier Conversations

Of course, I don't just mean conversations by the copy machine, but for the purposes of this book, we'll label those passerby conversations as "copier conversations." There's a limited amount of time we spend at the copier, waiting in the commons for an available restroom, exchanging small talk before or after meetings, or standing at classroom doors welcoming students in.

These small moments have so much potential, more than we realize. We have the opportunity to make these copier conversations meaningful instead of regular, mundane, or sometimes dreaded. If you're anything like me, you say almost exactly the same thing every time: "Hey, how's it going?" And the response? "Oh, it's going..." or "Good, how about you?" It's boring, right? But we don't have any other tools in our toolbox for making these conversations more meaningful. And most of the time, let's be honest, we don't see the point of making these small moments anything more than typical.

If we can make a small one-degree shift in our thinking about these copier conversations, we may start to see an uptick in the climate of our organization and, over time, even a shift in culture. A one-degree shift might take our "Hey, how's it going?" to "Hey, what's gone well so far today?" Or perhaps to, "Hey, what did you find helpful about using the new PLC agenda this morning?"

Check out the podcast episode *Leading with Curiosity* to find some practical tips for having more meaningful copier conversations.

Catching Up with Casey
Show on YouTube

Leading with Curiosity
with
Dr. Amy Mathews-Perez

Meeting Conversations

The conversations that happen inside a meeting don't stay in the meeting—they carry on into those smaller copier conversations, or maybe even into the lunchroom where venting and gossip tend to happen. That's why the conversations within meetings matter significantly. When they're well-run, they set a positive tone for everything that follows.

Leigh Epsy (2017) writes:

A poorly run meeting is a waste of time. There's the opportunity cost. Instead of sitting in a poorly run meeting, you could have been in a conversation generating reliable solutions, identifying next steps to move a project forward, or any number of valuable activities. (p. 8)

As you go through the Clarity Cycle Framework, it will be important to evaluate the meetings that typically happen throughout the week, month, or school year. What is happening during these meetings? Are the conversations life-giving, dialogical, and fostering productive talk once the meeting is over? Is the vision for this work being cast, conceived of, and caught by stakeholders during meetings? Are you noticing the vision being carried forward by those stakeholders outside the meeting?

How you lead meetings and facilitate conversations within them matters. When I take leaders through the *Meetings that Matter* training, they often walk away realizing that more than half the meetings they're having could be de-implemented, combined, flipped, or significantly adjusted.

Expect Adjustments

Speaking of adjustments, they're not just likely—they're inevitable. Throughout each step of the Clarity Cycle Framework, you'll find opportunities to tweak and refine the work you've done. Sometimes, you may even revisit entire steps to ensure everything remains aligned and effective. Some steps, however, seem to call for adjustments more often than others. Insight, vision, and celebrating—three of the most dynamic and challenging habits to build—require particular attention because they rely on factors that can shift or feel unpredictable.

Why are these steps so tricky? Don't forget: people are complex, and creating clarity for those people is equally complex. That's why I want to ensure you're prepared to adapt and leverage these habits effectively to calibrate and sustain progress. Let's dive into the kinds of adjustments you might need to consider for these three pivotal steps in the Clarity Cycle Framework.

Gaining Insight from Stakeholders

It's essential to cycle back to "gaining insight" regularly to maintain clarity and momentum. Think back to Chapter 6, where we discussed the importance of listening tours as a way to uncover patterns, celebrate wins, and reveal areas of confusion. These moments of reflection allow you to anchor the work in stakeholder experiences and keep the organization aligned to the area of focus and goals.

Consider scheduling intentional times throughout the year to revisit this step—not just to identify gaps but to celebrate accomplishments and reinforce accountability. When we consistently engage stakeholders, you'll maintain a pulse on their needs.

Scripting Critical Moves & Casting Vision

Critical moves are rarely set in stone; they need to be fluid enough to adapt to changing circumstances while staying aligned with the vision. Remember the Vision Curve from Chapter 7? Casting and recalibrating vision is an ongoing process, and sometimes it requires rethinking the critical moves that bring the vision to life. Reflect on whether some action steps need to be shifted to later in the year, postponed until next year, or even removed entirely to protect capacity and sustainability.

Insight from stakeholders and data should guide these decisions. For instance, if feedback from listening tours indicates that a particular critical move is overwhelming or ineffective, consider adjusting it to better serve your team. These tweaks ensure your team remains focused, empowered, and capable of achieving meaningful progress while maintaining their trust and commitment.

Providing Feedback & Celebrating Systematically

Take time to evaluate how well your systematic approach to feedback and celebration is working. As discussed in Chapter 8, celebrations can either energize and motivate or feel hollow and forced, depending on how intentional they are. What patterns are emerging? Are certain accomplishments consistently being celebrated while others are overlooked? Are all stakeholders being recognized, and how are they responding to those celebrations?

Feedback and celebration should be tied directly to the area of focus and goals, keeping them "top of mind," as we talked about earlier in this chapter. Regularly measuring progress and assessing the system's sustainability will allow you to pivot and make tweaks where necessary. Celebrating should energize and motivate your team, not feel like an additional burden.

When We Lose Our Way

Shocktober, the Holidays, Testing Season...

These are just a few of the times when it's all too easy to lose sight of the destination. We might take a wrong turn or find ourselves spinning in different directions, leaving our teams disoriented. Michael Fullan (2013) calls this phenomenon the "implementation dip," and he's right. But it's not necessarily a bad thing. Fullan explains that "*all successful schools experience implementation dips as they move forward*" (p. 40). It's a natural part of the process, not a reason to abandon ship but rather a signal to recalibrate.

The "implementation dip" reminds me of Elisabeth Kübler-Ross' Change Curve, developed in 1969 to depict the five stages of grief: denial, anger, bargaining, depression, and acceptance. While this model has been widely applied to various forms of change, it can feel a little dramatic when applied to clarity work in schools. So, I've developed a variation of this model that aligns more closely with the Clarity Cycle Framework, as shown in Figure 9.2.

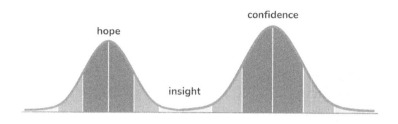

Figure 9.2

With any change, we all begin with a sense of hope—a belief in what could and should be. The same is true when we set out to create clarity in our organizations. After all, the purpose of clarity is to move away from the chaos of ambiguity and make real, tangible progress. But hope is only the starting point. Inevitably, we encounter what Fullan (2013) describes as the dip, and this is where the real work begins.

One leader I've worked with affectionately calls this phase "The Suck," borrowing language from Brené Brown (2018) to emphasize how difficult this stage can feel. While it's uncomfortable, it's also where insight is gained and meaningful growth begins. The key is to see this as part of the journey—an essential step on the climb toward confidence, commitment, and ultimately, sustainable progress. By reframing "The Suck" as an opportunity rather than a setback, you'll be better equipped to lead your teams out of the dip and toward confidence.

The question remains, though: is it worth it? I hope you wholeheartedly believe that it is. I hope you see that to gain confidence in yourself and to build capacity within your team, you'll embrace the challenging yet incredibly rewarding work of creating clarity.

Are you ready to embark on this journey?

It's time to perfect the craft of clarity!

Resources to Develop the Habit of Calibrating and Sustaining Progress

CALIBRATION PLANNING DOCUMENT

Reflection Questions:
-
-
-
-
-

Data Points to Evaluate Progress
-
-
-
-
-

Agenda :
- Purpose, Success Criteria, Norms
-
-
-
-
- Next Steps and Challenge

Adjustments and Justification

Casey Watts
COACHING & CONSULTING

"Yeah, but…What if?" Meets "Yeah, and…Could it be?"

If you've spent time in the intermundium—that in-between space where perspectives collide—you've likely felt the tension of misaligned narratives. Teachers and leaders see the same picture through different lenses. One group feels overloaded and unclear, while the other feels stuck and unheard. It's a frustrating place to live, and if we're not careful, it's easy to stay there.

That's where clarity comes in.

Inevitably, creating clarity will feel like too much work, too lofty, or perhaps even too idealistic. The steps you've read about in this book might seem unrealistic at first glance. But this is where I push back. I invite you to zoom out and ask yourself: Why are we doing this? What happens to student learning, teacher capacity, and organizational progress if we don't?

If we keep choosing products and programs over this work, will we ever see anything different? Or will we keep spinning on the same hamster wheel, solving the same problems over and over again?

"Yeah, but ... what if?"

As you sit with this framework, you'll likely find yourself leaning into familiar phrases that start with, "Yeah, but..."

- Yeah, but what if people resist?
- Yeah, but what if something deeper is uncovered?
- Yeah, but what if district leadership or the state piles on something else?
- Yeah, but what if we don't have enough time, people, or resources?

These are valid concerns—realities we often face. But here's the thing: if we let those concerns dominate, we'll never escape the cycle of doubt and stagnation.

"Yeah, and ... Could it be?"

Let's meet those "Yeah, but..." statements with a spirit of curiosity and possibility, turning them into "Yeah, and ... Could it be?"

- Yeah, we might face resistance...
  And could it be that resistance signals a need for greater clarity and mastery experiences?
- Yeah, something deeper might emerge...
  And could it be that uncovering deeper issues brings us closer to meaningful solutions?
- Yeah, resources feel limited...
  And could it be that a shared vision brings efficiency and focus to how we use what we have?

The truth is, clarity requires us to push past those doubts and embrace discomfort. You must hold onto the area of focus, stay steady with the vision, and give your people a framework that brings alignment to their work and purpose to their efforts.

I mention in the introduction, a desire to bridge the gap and move beyond misalignment to get to alignment and the kind of commitment that binds a team together, even when it feels hard. When we replace "Yeah, but..." with "Yeah, and..." we're rewriting the narrative. We're choosing to zoom out, see the bigger picture, and zoom back in to create a shared focus.

Even If...

Some may still scoff at your efforts. But clarity is not about appeasing the doubters or convincing the skeptics. Even if you run into this reality, you must stay true to the vision, believe in your people, and not allow the minority to derail the momentum of the majority. This work is about fostering habits like intentional feedback, systematic celebration, and calibrated adjustments—habits that sustain progress long after the initial spark of change has faded; habits that stay with YOU no matter what position you hold or where you are in life.

The work of clarity is not for the faint of heart, but it is for those who believe in something bigger than themselves. It's for leaders who want to leave teams better than they found them. It's for those willing to reflect, monitor, and adjust when things go off course, as they inevitably will.

As you move forward, my hope is that you'll hear fewer "Yeah, but..." voices—both internally and externally—and start hearing more, "Yeah, and... Could it be?" Because the power to move beyond the old story lies in the questions you choose to answer, the vision you dare to cast, and the progress you commit to sustaining.

You've got this. And your people are counting on you to be the leader who finally creates clarity.

Meet the Author

Casey Watts is the founder of Casey Watts Coaching & Consulting, LLC, and a Team Leadership Expert. She has over 20 years of experience in education as a classroom teacher, adjunct professor, academic coordinator, and district instructional specialist. She is passionate about empowering teams to move beyond silos and transform into cohesive, vision-driven powerhouses. Through strategic guidance and practical tools, Casey helps leaders cultivate clarity, collaboration, and a collective purpose that drives meaningful results.

With a Bachelor's in Interdisciplinary Studies and a Master's in Education from Stephen F. Austin State University, Casey has dedicated her career to fostering collective efficacy. She specializes in equipping educators and leaders with actionable strategies to close learning gaps, build teacher capacity, and enhance team dynamics. Her visionary approach and ability to ask the right questions spark transformation, helping teams identify their unique strengths and script the critical moves needed to achieve their goals.

In addition to her work with schools and organizations, Casey hosts *The Catching Up with Casey Podcast*, where she explores innovative approaches to leadership, shares insights on team building, and inspires listeners to lead with intention and impact. Whether facilitating workshops, speaking at conferences, or coaching leaders one-on-one, Casey is committed to helping teams unlock their full potential and create lasting change.

References

ASCD. (n.d.). *Designing strategic elementary schedules.* Retrieved [June 2024], from https://ascd.org/blogs/designing-strategic-elementary-schedules

Bandura, A. (1997). *Self-efficacy: The exercise of control.* W.H. Freeman and Company.

Brown, B. (2018). *Dare to lead: Brave work. Tough conversations. Whole hearts.* Random House.

Cacioppo, J. T., Cacioppo, S., & Gollan, J. K. (2014). The negativity bias: Conceptualization, quantification, and individual differences. *Behavioral and Brain Sciences, 37*(3), 309–310. https://doi.org/10.1017/S0140525X13002537

Clark, R. (2015). *Move your bus: An extraordinary new approach to accelerating success in work and life.* Touchstone.

Covey, S. R. (2013). *The 7 habits of highly effective people.* Free Press.

DeWitt, P. M. (2022). *De-implementation: Creating the space to focus on what works.* Corwin.

DuFour, R., & Fullan, M. (2013). *Cultures built to last: Systemic PLCs at work™.* Solution Tree.

Emberton M. (2021). Unconscious Bias Is a Human Condition. The Permanente journal, 25, 20.199. https://doi.org/10.7812/TPP/20.199

Espy, L. (2018). *Bad meetings happen to good people: How to run meetings that are effective, focused, and produce results.* Independently published.

Fullan, M. (2011). *Leading in a culture of change* (Updated ed.). Jossey-Bass.

Gruenert, S., & Whitaker, T. (2015). *School culture rewired: How to define, assess, and transform it.* ASCD.

Hattie, J. (1992). Measuring the effects of schooling. *The Australian Journal of Education, 36*(1), 5–13. https://doi.org/10.1177/000494419203600102

Hattie, J. (2023). *Visible learning: The sequel: A synthesis of over 2,100 meta-analyses relating to achievement.* Routledge.

Heath, C., & Heath, D. (2010). *Switch: How to change things when change is hard.* Broadway Books.

Kanold, T. D. (2011). *Five disciplines of PLC leaders.* Solution Tree.

Knight, J. (2015). *Better conversations: Coaching ourselves and each other to be more credible, caring, and connected.* Corwin.

Lencioni, P. M. (2022). *The 6 types of working genius: A better way to understand your gifts, your frustrations, and your team.* Matt Holt Books.

Loehr, J., & Schwartz, T. (2003). *The power of full engagement: Managing energy, not time, is the key to high performance and personal renewal.* Free Press.

Olsen, A.B. (2022, June). 4 common reasons strategies fail. *Harvard Business Review.* https://hbr.org/2022/06/4-common-reasons-strategies-fail

Pink, D. H. (2011). *Drive: The surprising truth about what motivates us.* Riverhead Books.

Maxwell, J. C. (2005). *The 360 degree leader: Developing your influence from anywhere in the organization.* Thomas Nelson.

McChrystal, S., Collins, T., Silverman, D., & Fussell, C. (2015). *Team of teams: New rules of engagement for a complex world.* Portfolio.

Miller, D. (2017). *Building a story brand: Clarify your message so customers will listen.* HarperCollins Leadership.

Muhammad, A., & Cruz, L. F. (2019). *Time for change: Four essential skills for transformational school and district leaders.* Solution Tree.

Scott, S. (2002). *Fierce conversations: Achieving success at work and in life, one conversation at a time.* Berkley.

Sinek, S. (2009). *Start with why: How great leaders inspire everyone to take action.* Portfolio.

Stanier, M. B. (2020). *The advice trap: Be humble, stay curious & change the way you lead forever.* Box of Crayons Press.

Stanier, M. B. (2016). *The coaching habit: Say less, ask more & change the way you lead forever.* Box of Crayons Press.

Stanley, A. (2007). *Making vision stick.* Zondervan.

Sunstein, C. R., & Hastie, R. (2015). *Wiser: Getting beyond groupthink to make groups smarter.* Harvard Business Review Press.

The Happiness Index. (n.d.). *Clarity: Understanding its impact through neuroscience.* Retrieved [June 2024], from https://thehappinessindex.com/neuroscience/themes/clarity /

Visible Learning. (n.d.). *Visible Learning MetaX.* Retrieved [September 2024], from https://www.visiblelearningmetax.com/

Wexler, N. (2019). *The knowledge gap: The hidden cause of America's broken education system—and how to fix it.* Avery.

Wiseman, L., Allen, L. N., & Foster, E. (2013). *The multiplier effect: Tapping the genius inside our schools.* Corwin.